JOY'S EDGE

JOY'S EDGE

Transforming your life through mindfulness, wisdom, and compassion

Robin King

authorHOUSE®

AuthorHouse™ LLC
1663 Liberty Drive
Bloomington, IN 47403
www.authorhouse.com
Phone: 1-800-839-8640

Published by AuthorHouse 09/11/2014

ISBN: 978-1-4969-3464-2 (sc)
ISBN: 978-1-4969-3465-9 (e)

This book is printed on acid-free paper.

Because of the dynamic nature of the Internet, any web addresses or links contained in this book may have changed since publication and may no longer be valid. The views expressed in this work are solely those of the author and do not necessarily reflect the views of the publisher, and the publisher hereby disclaims any responsibility for them.

Additional materials

Additional materials, such as audio recordings of meditations and supplemental exercises, are available on my website, at http://www.joysedge.com/resources.

"*Joy's Edge* **contains all you need to transform your life from the inside out**. Combining ancient truths from the world's spiritual traditions with contemporary scientific research, Ms. King offers you grounded but powerful tools for aligning your life with your deepest spiritual yearnings. Each chapter explores a different step in this process, and includes detailed exercises for putting it into practice. **Every page shines with the energy of true awakening, wisdom, and happiness. A gem!**"

—*Lisa Erickson*,
Author of *Women's Energetics*,
Buddhism editor for *BellaOnline.com*, and
founder of the women's spirituality blog *Mommy Mystic*

"If you know in your heart that we are meant to live a life of joy and meaning, but you are not currently experiencing either at the level you desire, I highly recommend reading *Joy's Edge*. It is a beautiful balance of various teachings and modalities weaved in with the author's own life experiences. **Robin King offers simple practical tools you can implement right away, no matter where you are on life's path, to live the highest expression of you.**"

—*Mark Porteous*,
Author of *The Human Experience* and
co-founder of *Max Your Life, LLC*

"Robin King's writing is very clear and I love the personal examples she gives. **I hope to implement some of the techniques myself, and I feel that mindfulness may help some of my patients dealing with emotional pain** in a very unconscious fashion. They usually present with somatic complaints, stress, insomnia, etc… and want a pill to make it all go away. Some are lucky enough to find and be able to afford a good therapist, but for the rest a book like this may be very helpful."

—Yana Finkelshteyn, MD

"**I was so inspired by this book!** Robin King is able to weave introspective exercises, anecdotes and philosophy into a beautifully crafted narrative that was a pleasure to read. Chapters and topics in the book flowed effortlessly and purposefully. *Joy's Edge* **gave me perspective and relevance for my own life, without being preachy or judgmental.** As a skeptic of life coaching/self-improvement books in general, imagine my surprise at not being able to put this one down (even from my tiny iPhone screen)! I am grateful for having read this book, and for the gentle push to strive for joy in my life. I congratulate my extremely talented cousin Robin for finding her passion in writing. **This book has universal appeal and I highly recommend it to all!**"

—Rachel Merva

"*Joy's Edge* is a personable guide to transformation. Robin King is a gifted writer, able to encapsulate the core components of mindfulness, acceptance, and compassion. **The powerful exploration exercises provide a practical roadmap to living an authentic life.**"

—Mark Miesel, PhD, Sport and Performance Psychologist

About the Cover

The hawk has strong vision. It can see a rabbit from a mile away; it can see a mouse from 100 feet in the air. Because of its remarkable perception, the hawk is a symbol of insight, of seeing the bigger picture and our relationship to it. The hawk is also associated with spiritual paths, as perceptive gifts provide a means to see your situation truly, and to chart an effective course towards a life that resonates authentically with your spirit. The hawk inspires us to fly high, to soar towards our highest potential with power and grace.

May all recognize their own radiant awareness.
—Samantabhadra's prayer—

Disclaimer

The information provided in this book is designed to provide helpful information on the subjects discussed. This book should not be used to diagnose or treat any medical or psychological condition. For diagnosis or treatment of any medical problem, consult your own physician. The publisher and author are not responsible for any specific health needs that may require medical supervision and are not liable for any damages or negative consequences from any treatment, action, application, or preparation, to any person reading or following the information in this book. Any references included are provided for informational purposes only and do not constitute endorsement of any websites or other sources. Readers should be aware that any websites listed in this book might change.

Contents

Foreword

In my thirty plus years of serving as a family and hospice doctor, psychotherapist, and speaker on Near-Death Experiences, I've seen how frequently people live lives of external busyness until they are faced with a life-altering diagnosis. When life suddenly seems finite, many people examine their lives for the first time. That examination often reveals a life without meaning. Deeper exploration is needed to discover what does have meaning for them. That exploration is a turning point in their lives, whether or not the medical diagnosis ultimately leads to death. Many express regrets that they hadn't done that exploration earlier in life. It would have resulted in a fuller, more conscious life.

Joy's Edge offers structure to deep exploration of your life, whether you face a life-altering diagnosis or not. Robin King uses her own wisdom from a life deeply explored as well as Buddhist, Hindu, and psychotherapy philosophies to give you a framework to explore your own life deeply. Personal stories, philosophy, and exercises combine to deepen the experience.

The opportunities for personal explorations found in the book bring you from merely agreeing (or disagreeing) with the author into your own felt experience. In a gentle way, Robin King invites you to examine your own deeply held beliefs—not only the ones that you talk about, but also the ones that you act on in an unconscious manner. Never flinching, but always compassionate, *Joy's Edge* gives you opportunities to embrace your shadow, bring it to the light, and ultimately experience loving acceptance of every aspect of yourself, resulting in living life more fully.

I challenge you to read *Joy's Edge*, work the exercises, and let the wisdom permeate your life. I guarantee you will be changed, as I was changed.

PAMELA M. KIRCHER, MD
Author of *Love is the Link: A Hospice Doctor Shares her Experience of Near-Death and Dying*

In Gratitude

I am immensely grateful for the teachers that have blessed my life, especially my root meditation teacher. I am tremendously appreciative of my mom, who has been a powerful example of shaping a life following Spirit. She has also been an exceptional sounding board throughout my life, and especially in the creation of this book. I thank all others in my dear family as well, especially for serving as lovely examples of authentic living. I am so thankful for my spiritual sisters, for whom I feel deep love—for sharing their spiritual adventures, authenticity, and wisdom. In particular, I am thankful for Lisa, a wonderful writer who reviewed a late version of this text and provided valuable feedback. I am so grateful to have found my Love, Mark. I am hugely appreciative of all that he is, and for his incredible support for me, including his support for heart projects that I know don't always make logical or financial sense. He encourages me always to trust and follow my heart, and I am so grateful for that support, and for Mark being Mark. As well, I am continually blessed by the creatures in my life who have taught me powerful lessons in acceptance, presence, and mindful living. In the creation of this book, I am grateful for the insights and feedback from my editor, Judi. As well, I am enormously appreciative of proofreading by friends and family, in particular by my sharp-eyed Aunt Charlotte. Thank you!

THE BROAD VIEW

Joy's Edge

Knowledge is an unending adventure
at the edge of uncertainty.
—Jacob Bronowski—

Life as edge creatures

Back in college, I loved studying ecology. One tidbit I found fascinating had to do with the types of habitats that creatures seek. Some animals prefer to live in the center of an ecosystem, such as the heart of a rainforest or deep in the ocean, while others prefer to live where two or more ecosystems meet, such as on a coast or at the edge of a clearing. My professor pointed out that people seem to belong to this second lot: the edge creatures. We seek out shorelines—whether along rivers or oceans—and are willing to pay quite a premium for these edge habitats. Where edges don't exist, we create them: when we move into forests we cut down trees, and when we move to clearings, we plant them.

In the context of self-development, our love for edges can be quite useful. In yoga, sometimes we talk about *finding your edge*. The idea is that people generally have a comfort zone. In running, the comfort zone may be the speed that allows easy conversation. In stretching, it's the place you can reach without experiencing change over time. In careers, it's the level of advancement that requires no studying or planning outside the work day. In raising children, it's disengaged parenting, where you go through the motions—absentmindedly meeting physical needs without nurturing your child's spirit or engaging your child's mind. The comfort zone differs among people. And, for each of us, it changes both throughout a day and throughout a lifetime.

It may seem easy to rest in the comfort zone—but, ironically, it is *not*, in the long run, comfortable at all. We may imagine that being deep within the comfort "habitat" feels good, but when we are honest, we can see that life without growth and exploration can be quite boring. In fact, if you always stay within your comfort zone, your skills often diminish and your comfort zone shrinks. We are happier living where we are sufficiently challenged to support learning and growth without being so challenged as to feel overwhelmed. We feel best when we are discovering and expanding our edges.

So, in yoga, we talk about finding the edge, the place where we are challenged, but not stressed. For example, a person beginning a jogging regimen may run a few blocks to start, increasing the distance as endurance builds. A person building flexibility consciously discovers his stretching comfort zone and then reaches just a little beyond it. Reach too far, and injury is likely. But, reach just beyond what is easy, and flexibility improves. In our careers, we keep up with changes in our industries, studying in our spare time. We may keep our eyes open for midlife career shifts, and we do the work to support whatever area we feel we should grow. In parenting, we are actively engaged in utilizing *teaching moments* to encourage discovery. By seeking out the edges, we support exploration, growth, and, consequently, joy.

It is possible for you to live an awakened life—attending to your opportunities for growth in each moment, each day, each week, each month, and each year. I firmly believe that each of us feels much more fulfilled when we actively seek out our edges, and walk on our *just right* paths. So many of us struggle with feelings of disconnection between parts of our selves, or within our families, communities, or environments. Living authentically at joy's edge is about accepting where you are, while also creating and living a life that you love. It is about honoring all your parts—valuing and integrating your emotional, physical, social, mental, spiritual, familial, and economic lives; embracing your gifts and your shadows, and living a life with open eyes—gently, compassionately, and authentically engaged in becoming more deeply and beautifully aligned with who you really are.

My starting point

As a child, I was always studious. I loved exploring and learning, and I enjoyed going to school so much that I signed up for the daily before-school arts classes my elementary school offered. In high school, my concerned mom once asked about the load of homework that I powered through each night. I remember thinking it was a strange question, and I explained to her that I typically supplemented class assignments with additional readings. In college at the University of California at Berkeley, I was excited by the increased workload, and by the opportunity to talk about varied subjects with graduate students and professors who were truly energized by learning and exploring. I studied a wide range of subjects as I meandered through fields of interest—anthropology, biology, spirituality, Native American studies, art, and more. Luckily, all that work in high school paid off; I started college with nearly a year's worth of credits with advanced placement exams. I was able to graduate in four years with a major in biology (with an emphasis in ecology) and a minor in Native American studies.

My most essential and long-lasting discovery in college began with a free meditation class. From that first class, I was hooked. I was surprised and thrilled with the energy I experienced when meditating with a well-seasoned meditator, and I enthusiastically developed a meditative practice with the engaged support of a teacher who truly embodied compassionate wisdom. Over the many years since graduation, mindfulness and meditation have been essential elements in my life, and they have enriched it immeasurably. I am deeply grateful to the teachers with whom I studied directly and who revealed incredible beauty and depth of understanding along my path. In particular, I am grateful to my root meditation teacher—a Buddhist who provided innumerable opportunities to expose and work with my edges. He blessed my life in countless ways by embodying enlightened activity and mindful living, transmitting powerful teachings, and expanding my view of possibilities in the ten years I studied with him before his passing.

In addition to studying with living meditation teachers, I've also studied spiritual texts from a variety of cultures and religions, and have applied the teachings that resonated with me. As well, in college, I discovered the complementary practices of yoga and martial arts, and discovered that both practices were incredibly beneficial to me. In my twenties, I practiced martial arts regularly, often training a few hours a day, six or seven days a week. As I grew older, I expanded my yoga practice, and tapered martial arts training when I found that yoga felt more nourishing for me in my thirties and now my forties.

In my twenties, I developed a career in technology, and worked my way into computer consulting in New York City. I found it was a good fit for me. There were always opportunities for problem solving and for learning new technologies, it was lucrative, and I typically had regular hours that made it easy to maintain my meditation and martial arts practices. Throughout my business life, I found innumerable daily opportunities to apply lessons in mindfulness to my fast-paced working environments. I had a very lucky life.

Over time, however, a quiet voice gradually grew louder and more insistent, urging me to move west. A month shy of my thirtieth birthday, my dogs and I headed out to Colorado. After a few fits and starts, including a few months looking for work, and a few years working for a technology start-up that was on the brink of failure, I found steady employment as a computer consultant when the start-up was purchased and successfully resurrected under a new name.

My changing point

I love Colorado, and I was tremendously appreciative of my new, quieter home with much easier access to nature. I was also grateful for steady employment after my initial financial struggles after the move. At the same time, however, my life felt pretty out of balance. I was working as a traveling consultant, sleeping more often in hotel rooms than in my own bed. It was a life that would be suitable for a lot of people—it paid well, my contributions were valued, and I traveled to many places I would not have otherwise visited. I have never been married, but my roommate was a friend who cared for my dogs while I traveled in exchange for free rent, and I had quality time with my dogs on the weekends.

Knowing how stressful it was not to know how I'd make ends meet, I was thankful to have steady work. I knew that the amount of stress, travel, and time away from my dogs and home were all taking their toll. My dogs were my dear family, and I felt heavy-hearted about the amount of time we spent apart. I knew intuitively that I wasn't living the life that was most aligned with my spirit.

I was doing the basic self-healing techniques so many of us do—getting daily exercise and meditation, going for hikes on weekends, taking baths in essential oils, eating organic foods, and drinking herbal teas. And yet, the deeper part of me knew that those efforts were insufficient, and that I needed to reorganize my life in a fundamental way to genuinely meet my personal needs—and to be truer to myself. Even so, I was so fearful of losing the security that the position provided that I chose not to look too closely at how far out of alignment my life had become.

Until...

I continued in this way for a few years, knowing that I wasn't on my authentic path and that I was ignoring my spirit's call for change, because I was fearful of being financially stressed. Against my better judgment, I hoped that my modest attempts towards balance would somehow suffice. That is, I overlooked my doubts until one of my dear middle-aged dogs, Mushin, was unexpectedly diagnosed with a terminal illness and given two to six months to live. While I know that some people feel affection towards pets that falls somewhat below their favorite pair of jeans, for *me*, my dogs were family. I took the prognosis the way many people would receive news of a terminal condition in their child.

Suddenly, I felt the immediacy of each decision in my life. While my lifestyle had seemed "good enough" before the diagnosis, my view changed fundamentally when I realized that my dear friend would likely be gone in a few short months. Every aspect of my life came under the microscope, and the parts of my personality that were willing to ignore misalignments were blessedly silenced.

I quickly let the company know that I would be unable to travel while Mushin was alive, as the care required to ensure quality of life was not something I could entrust to someone else. I offered to do whatever was best for the company—resign, take a leave of absence, or work remotely whenever remote work was available. As it turned out, they opted to provide remote work, and throughout my time with them, I always had sufficient income. Unexpectedly, the parts of my job that felt in conflict with my spirit disappeared, and the parts that I loved remained. I felt incredibly fortunate, and grateful.

Just after the diagnosis, I studied a few books on energy healing and practiced their exercises. Then, I approached my canine friend and began doing the first energy exercise (holding my hands a few inches away from his body). Mushin was quite the cuddler, and was always ready for belly rubs and ear scratches. However, he looked at me with an exasperated expression and moved a few feet out of range. I moved towards him, petted him for a few minutes, and then tried once again. Again, he moved away. The message I got that day was that the tumor wasn't something I was supposed to *fix* or to *will away*. Rather, it offered me the opportunity to provide it unconditional love and to welcome it into our lives, regardless of the changes its presence would require. I cried as I sat near my canine friend, and we had a good long cuddle that his brother quickly joined.

The vet was right about the diagnosis, and about the typical life expectancy, but Mushin exceeded even the most optimistic projections, living over four years more (and into his senior years). Even better, he lived with high spirits and energy that had him enjoying one or two daily walks, eager leaps into the backseat, and regular trail hikes and visits to the park—even enjoying a peaceful autumn stroll through the park on what we knew had to be his last day (as he was at last exhibiting the symptoms that signaled an upcoming rapid decline in quality of life).

Since I never knew when he would go, I felt naturally drawn to enjoy every moment more mindfully than before the diagnosis. He was diagnosed in June, and we celebrated the first whiff of autumn breeze in August. As he passed small milestones—the equinox, his birthday, Christmas Eve (the 7th anniversary of his joining our family), the New Year—the dogs and I celebrated with meditation, hiking, and belly rubs.

By traveling less, I had time to deepen my yoga practice, eventually earning a 200 hour certification to teach yoga. I also lost a fair amount of weight, and felt healthier than I had in years. Although I frequently experienced insomnia when traveling, I found my natural sleep cycle returned when I spent more time at home. I found a second career that aligned well with my growing interest in health and well-being, and had time to take prerequisite classes through the local university and the community college. Eventually, I was able to make a bigger shift, earning a Master of Science degree in occupational therapy, a healing profession I discovered during this period of renewal.

Once I aligned my life towards wellness, my mind and body found balance, and ease was a welcome by-product. However, it is important to understand that the crucial aspect wasn't that I oriented towards a healing practice or that I sought ease. Rather, the essential process was accepting where I was, identifying my own authentic path, and then living it with compassion and disciplined attention. Even though my shift in profession required several years of training, simply heading in a more authentic direction generated deep feelings of peace, happiness, and fulfillment.

I learned from my experience that walking an authentic path requires us to summon the courage, discipline, and persistence to take steps into the unknown, trusting we are launching a cascade of changes that will lead us to opportunities for personal growth, even—or, more truly, *especially*—when we feel the discomfort of our own edges. The key ingredients for transformation are: acceptance of what is actually present in your life, wisdom to discern where change is needed, and compassion for yourself and others as you negotiate the bumps along your path of transformation.

I don't want to give the impression that, once I made a shift, everything fell neatly into place. Finding your edge and living your truth are not processes of linear progress towards fixed goals. Rather, they are active processes that require vigilant, meticulous attention as you spiral into beauty and depth. Being aware of your own unique place of greatest opportunity and living from your truth requires mindfulness and continual re-assessment.

I've found that self-discovery is a lot like surfing: success requires dedicated, focused observation, paddling hard once you see your goal, and being ready to resume vigilance after every brief, blissful moment of riding a wave, feeling integrated with the ocean. Naturally, I still have days when I'm knocked off my board. But, I also know that those moments provide tremendous invitations to explore the ocean more deeply. Fortunately, when you skillfully employ tools to help you as you walk your path, the process becomes deeper and more rewarding.

Empowering your path

It's pretty common for us to think that life circumstances, or our current health, is "good enough." While we might be aware of some negatives, a lot of us are unwilling to do what it takes to honestly appraise and adjust those aspects of our lives that are not aligned with our needs and gifts. For me, and for many people, it takes some sort of crisis—unemployment, diagnosis, divorce—to force us to honestly appraise where we are and where an authentic life would take us.

And yet, there is no need to wait for catastrophe; you can make a choice in any moment to live from your truth. The truth is, I was letting my fear of financial instability overshadow my quiet, yet insistent inner voice that demanded change. A point of crisis made my financial fears seem insignificant and forced me to re-align my life. But honest reflection could have pointed me in the same direction much sooner, had I been willing to look at my needs more honestly and my circumstances more creatively.

If you are willing to stop, evaluate your life and path, explore your edge, and make changes in service to your ultimate well-being, you are in a wonderful space to start. My well-being was honestly not enough of a drive for me to be willing to risk financial stress. It was only when my canine friend needed my help that I felt compelled to evaluate and realign my life in service to wellness.

Maybe you are like me, in that you commit yourself more fully to healing when you do so in service to someone or something you feel is greater than yourself. During the time I was making my biggest shifts towards a more authentic path, *I* was never the conscious reason for the change. Instead, I made shifts towards a more authentic, joyful life in order to bring more healing energy into our home, reducing stress and supporting my canine friend's well-being. Even though I actually made conscious choices for self-healing, I did so in service to my dog's optimal health.

Many of us who won't summon the drive to heal for ourselves can find the will power to do so out of love for our children, for our significant others, for God, for art, or for some cause that expresses our soul's purpose. There are things we are willing to do, risks we are willing to take, walls we are willing to break through, out of love for someone or something that we perceive as greater than ourselves. For me, an imminent death served as an urgent reminder to attend to that which is truly essential—and that which is most closely aligned with my own essence. If you aren't already doing all you can for optimal wellness, perhaps you would benefit from reflecting on what you love enough to be willing to face any truth, however painful, and to make any change, however difficult, in order to truly heal and grow.

Personal Exploration #1: Reflection for inspiration

I invite you to take some time to reflect on your deepest, most heart-felt inspiration for living an authentic life. What do you love so much you that are willing to change? As you reflect, don't worry about finding the *right* answer; there isn't one. Instead, open to your intuition. You may start by considering such questions as:

- What is the one thing that is most likely to cause me to wake with a smile on my face, eager to start my day?
- What makes me smile when I think about it, even in the midst of a rough afternoon?
- What, when it passes through my thoughts, makes my heart glow?
- Whom do I feel called to serve? There are many possible answers here, and many beautiful possibilities, such as your God, your children, your spouse, or people with whom you feel the kinship of a common struggle. The essential challenge is to identify what answer truly resonates with you.
- If you come up with something abstract, such as *to be rich*, deepen your reflection to identify specifics. What does more money mean for you? Travel? A larger home? Luxurious surroundings? More time with family? Freedom to follow your passion? Similarly, if you are inspired by being healthier, what does *health* really mean for you? Less pain throughout your day? More energy to follow a passion, or to play with your children or grandchildren? An active, adventurous lifestyle? Feeling beautiful?
- It's also possible you've already found your muse. Has there been a time when you were trying to accomplish something important and you faced a block, but then inspiration gave you seemingly superhuman strength, allowing you to break through? See if you can remember what that inspiration was.

Give yourself as much time as you need to get in touch with whatever it is that you love and value so much that it inspires you to align more beautifully with your truest version of yourself, regardless of the difficulties entailed. Listen to your heart and to your gut, rather than to your *ideas* of what the answer *should* be.

Once you have identified your personal wellspring of inspiration, you might want to find a visual representation of it to place in a prominent place. Perhaps you'll have a picture of loved ones in the office or in a locket for those moments when you need to re-center yourself on your path. There are endless variations on this theme, such as a keychain talisman reminding you of a place you would like to travel, a piece of jewelry with stones or symbols representing the source of your inspiration, or a picture of a deity, saint, or teacher who inspires you. Place your object wherever you most need the inspiration or, if appropriate, wear it everywhere you go. Think creatively, since your answers are uniquely your own.

Remember to look at your representation whenever you need motivation. One tendency I've noticed is that, over time, we tend to stop noticing static objects. So, if my inspirational image isn't catching my eye, I might move the postcard or photo to a different place, get a different frame, or even rotate a few related inspiring images in the frame so that my mind is more likely to register them. I also remind myself to return to my source of inspiration whenever I find myself procrastinating on doing something I know I need to do.

An Authentic Path

We keep moving forward, opening new doors, and doing new things,
because we're curious and curiosity keeps leading us down new paths.
—*Walt Disney*—

There are quick paths and long paths

In the years that I've studied a variety of western psychology and spiritual paths, I've noticed that one way to categorize them is *quick paths* versus *long paths*. Both of these paths have histories within a variety of traditions, and both can be useful in self-discovery. Within religious systems, long paths are more commonly (though not exclusively) associated with lay people. Long paths emphasize regularly attending services, volunteering, tithing, and following rules or commandments. In contrast, through the ages, many monks, nuns, and mystics have gravitated towards quick-path practices. Quick paths emphasize deep introspection, conscious reflection, and enlightened activity. On a quick path, one's whole life is utilized in service to discovery and deepening personal connection with truth, love, and the divine. Quick paths invite us to deeply explore what it means to live an awakened, authentic life.

The long path takes (as you might expect) a lot longer to reach the same levels of peace and understanding. The quick path is much faster—though it also takes more discipline, attention, and effort, and it can at times be quite uncomfortable. The long path can be viewed as climbing a mountain by spiraling slowly up it, plodding along and adding altitude gradually. The quick path is similar to running up the side of the mountain like a goat, increasing altitude as fast as possible.

The long path covers more ground; the quick path is shorter and more efficient, but requires more energy and focus. The paths are, however, equivalent in that following either to its end gets you to the top of the mountain.

There's a well-known story in Buddhist oral tradition about a monk who sees a scorpion in a pond, scoops it out to safety, and is stung in the process. The scorpion falls back into the water; the monk scoops it out again, and is again stung. After several attempts at saving the scorpion, the monk's baffled companion asks why he continues to rescue the scorpion when it continues to hurt him in return. The monk replies, "It is the scorpion's nature to sting. It is my nature to help others. Eventually, I'll stop feeling the pain of the sting, or he'll stop being afraid and stinging. Either way, he'll be saved." I see that monk as a seeker on a long path.

On a quick path, instead of enduring the same pain again and again, you truly stop and investigate the source of your suffering. What you find is that, even though pain exists, it is really your *reaction* to pain that creates suffering. On a quick path, you notice where you hurt, and you study its root cause. You investigate yourself with love—and without blame or excuses—to see whether some activity of mind or body is creating unnecessary suffering. A quick-path monk would investigate his pain, understand the source of it, and realize that he can help the scorpion without getting hurt, that he can be comfortable whether or not the scorpion changes, and that there is no need to terrorize the scorpion in order to rescue it. The quick-path monk would simply get a branch or a big leaf (or the tail of his robe, or his bowl, if no vegetation were nearby) to ferry the scorpion to safety.

As a teenager, I worked some summers and holidays in a psychotherapist's office. As I prepared her patients' records for their charts, I found that nearly all required the same rubber stamp, *Adjustment Reaction to Adulthood.* At the time, it seemed very strange to me that people well into adulthood would still be adjusting to a status they had reached decades before. When I asked my mom (a physician and fellow psychotherapist) about it, she said that none of these people had defined mental illnesses. They were simply people who were disappointed with how their lives had started, or how they had turned out, or the life choices they had made. These people shared common, recurring issues with anger, resentment, sadness, shame, guilt, regret—the whole gamut of negative emotions. They typically visited their psychotherapist every week or two for years, working on their issues through a process of talk therapy. These clients were, from my perspective, on a long path. This sort of long-path talk therapy can be incredibly beneficial to some people, depending on their personalities and challenges. As well, when people are working through trauma, a slower pace may feel less threatening.

There are also quick-path styles in psychotherapy, such as transformational psychology and cognitive-behavioral psychology, where significant gains are expected within weeks or months. Because unaddressed issues can typically be observed as recurring patterns with different people playing similar roles, a psychotherapist operating from the perspective of a quick path would more likely guide clients to see their own patterns, make peace with the past, and actively work to establish new, healthier ways of thinking, interacting, and living in the world. The quick-path therapist would likely be working towards quickly rendering himself or herself unnecessary—while staying busy, as their success brings in new clients.

While quick-path therapists may help clients to reach their goals in a matter of weeks, it is also possible to work with a single guide on a quick path over a number of years. For example, many monks spend a lifetime benefiting from the guidance of a single, quick-path spiritual teacher. When this method works, providing insights that build on insights, it does so because of the guidance the teacher provides by persistently shining a light on the student's edges. The practitioner explores and expands his edges, simultaneously growing into deeper and deeper resonance with truth and stillness (instead of simply exploring the same issues at roughly the same level of understanding).

We can visualize the tool a long-path seeker uses as something like an archeologist's soft brush, an instrument used to softly sweep away thousands of years of grime to reveal carved stone. After a careful dusting, the archeologist meticulously studies every marking for its meaning: *Is that water or wind erosion? Is that a word or a sacred symbol? Something purely decorative or ceremonial?* The person on a long path studies his personal history, believing it has tremendous value in itself. He may consciously or unconsciously re-interpret past events to create stronger, better, wiser versions of *me*.

On the other hand, the person on a quick path isn't motivated by learning more about the stone or the subtleties of its carvings. She is not nearly so interested in reviewing or re-framing incidents of the past as she is in diving deeply into an exploration of the present. The quick-path explorer's instrument is a pick ax, which is used to break through rocks to reveal diamonds hidden within. The quick-path person pounds away to find buried jewels. She expects the process to be sweaty and messy, and believes that stories are not to be studied but broken through to reveal the spiritual diamonds that are found as the mechanisms of ego are progressively exposed and discarded.

Common elements of a long path from a religious or spiritual standpoint include attending weekly meetings, being pleasant to others, donating to charities, and so on. The path often has an outward focus, and there may be a tendency to dwell on the behavior of others. There may be some attention to the ways in which our personality can be improved to elicit better reactions from others. Although the long path may entail limited introspection, it doesn't require nearly so much deep exploration and dissection of the structures of the egoic mind as the quick path. It's a fairly comfortable path, and people on it are more or less content. Transformation is generally slow and measured.

By contrast, the person on a spiritual quick path sees everything as holy, and uses every aspect of her life to expose and release aspects of the ego. While she values and honors interactions and relationships with others, she is not focused on outward forms. The elements of her mind and life that create discomfort are identified and explored with courage, honesty, and compassion. Instead of accepting her life as "good enough," she investigates deeply and honestly, discovering and walking her own unique path. As she gets into her groove, she develops an increased awareness for the places in her life where she *burns*—where she feels the unmistakable friction that arises when she is misaligned with her spirit's path. Instead of creating excuses, or beating herself up, she gazes unflinchingly and invites her mind to deeply, and then more deeply, explore these *hot spots*. Most importantly, she then creates mindful and compassionate space around them.

I think of the quick path as *healing with light*—as shining light into the shadows, and truly, honestly, and fundamentally discovering that there is nothing to fear. The quick path teaches us that nothing needs to be grasped or avoided, including (or, perhaps, especially) our definitions of ourselves. Gradually, the (often unconscious) ideas that obstruct our path become apparent and then dissolve, and we naturally flow into greater resonance with our truth. Since our fears and aversions sometimes kick up a lot of dirt on the quick path, we can expect to feel some emotional discomfort as we confront them. But we can also expect to experience blissful highs as the exposed egoic structures dissolve, and the indescribable joy of freedom floods our being.

I'm writing this book as a person who loves the quick path and who wants to share what I've learned about walking the quick path with you. I do, however, want to emphasize that a quick path is not the "right" way for self-discovery. Quick paths and long paths are both potentially tremendously beneficial aids in personal and spiritual growth, and different personalities benefit from different approaches. A quick path is simply one valuable way to grow. The practices presented in these pages invite you to leap joyfully into your own particular quick path. They provide a means by which you can open space to discover and live your unique, authentic life. While walking a long path may support you in making gradual changes over years, sprinting on a quick path allows you to sift through lifetimes of mental debris as your tightly focused intent allows painful thoughts to fall away.

Living authentically at joy's edge

Quick paths, as well as long paths, can focus outwardly, albeit with a few essential differences. Most importantly, your fundamental focus on a quick path is on inner work, and your outer work complements inner discoveries. Living authentically on joy's edge begins with creating and cultivating a field of compassionate acceptance for yourself and for everyone in your life. Acceptance goes much further than mere tolerance. It grants the freedom to shine a loving light on the parts you resist as well as the parts you like; it is essential for nourishing the equanimity that grows into deep, abiding gratitude and joy. In this rich ground of acceptance, wisdom finds the nourishment it needs to take root. You grow wise by developing the capacity to discern without being judgmental. Further, when you create a field of acceptance and permeate it with your wisdom's true seeing, you develop the ability to speak and live your truth with courage and love, and with trust in your authentic path. You embody an active, powerful, transformative, compassionate presence.

At joy's edge, you begin by diving deeply, and then more deeply, into authentic loving awareness and acceptance for whatever life brings. As this acceptance deepens, it blossoms into genuine gratitude for everything you encounter on your path. As the Dalai Lama said, "In the practice of tolerance, one's enemy is the best teacher." The practice of acceptance is about letting go of the notion that you need your outer world to look any particular way in order for you to be deeply, truly, happy. This practice provides profound, humbling, heart-opening lessons in gratitude, compassion, and stillness.

So often in life, we create dis-ease by wishing things were somehow different. If only you had a different body, a different job, a different spouse, different past choices, different thought patterns, or any other example of life's circumstances, you could be a *new, better you*, you would be *worthy* of love, or health, or peace, or exuberance… and you could therefore be happy.

There is a well-known Taoist folk tale that highlights the peace and balance that arise when life is met with acceptance. This story began with a Taoist farmer's only horse running away. His neighbors consoled him, saying that the loss was bad luck. He shrugged, smiled, and said it's impossible to know whether luck is good or bad. A month later, his horse returned and brought with it two strong wild horses. His neighbors exclaimed that he was so lucky to have three healthy horses, and the farmer simply shrugged and smiled, saying it's impossible to see whether luck is good or bad. A few days later, the farmer's only son was thrown from one of the wild horses and broke his leg. Once more, the villagers consoled the farmer for his bad luck. And again, the farmer shrugged, smiled, and said that luck is neither good nor bad. A few weeks later, the army came to the village to recruit all service-aged boys and men for battle. Since the farmer's son had a broken leg, he was the only young man left behind. The villagers were amazed at the farmer's good luck, but he simply shrugged, smiled, and said *it is what it is*.

We can see where we accept and resist reality in a variety of ways. Physically, when acceptance guides our life, we may have a welcoming smile, an easy step, and a ready laugh. In contrast, when resistance guides us, we may develop frown lines, ulcers, stooping shoulders, and migraines. Mentally, when we live with acceptance, we feel optimistic, engaged, and loving. On the other hand, when we live with resistance, we may feel anxious, angry, or depressed. Spiritually, when we accept reality, we see the universe as mysterious, beautiful, and rich with possibility. On the other hand, resistance may drive us to view life as hostile, deficient, and ugly. When we develop acceptance for whatever is present *right now* (without committing to a static, inauthentic life), when we commit to the view that, *in this moment, everything is okay*, we develop the means by which to experience the beauty that is always present—the beauty the world continuously presents in unexpected ways.

The practice of acceptance teaches you that you can be truly joyful regardless of circumstances so long as you truly welcome life *just as it is*. You have a choice to let go of your stories about how things could be and, especially, *should* be. You have the choice to stop struggling against your thoughts or believing your thoughts. When you choose spacious acceptance, you experience a joy that is too subtle to notice when all of those ideas about *what's wrong* go zipping around, clouding your field of vision.

The power of living on joy's edge—of working on the edge of discomfort—is this: you discover that challenging situations give you opportunities to dig more deeply, revealing that you have the power to choose your reactions. You are truly not dependent on having things go as you think they should in order to be deeply and profoundly happy. You have the power to simply witness thoughts without claiming them as true, or arguing against them. In this recognition and allowing, the light you shine on your thoughts dissolves their fierce hold on your mind. Moreover, in meeting the world with loving acceptance, you discover that your own open heart soothes and awakens others, creating unimagined possibilities.

Enlisting acceptance as the ground for authentic living

When taken too far, the practice of acceptance can lead to a counterproductive paralysis. Acceptance on an authentic path does not imply that you should always follow the course of least resistance. One objection to the practice of acceptance might be expressed as, "He who goes with the flow goes down the drain." I remember once hearing American spiritual teacher Gangaji talk about a spiritual teacher who received a letter from a person living above a 24-hour mechanic shop. Because of the constant noise, he hadn't had good sleep or meditation at home for as long as he could remember. He felt like he was approaching his wit's end, and wrote asking for advice. The teacher asked his students how they would respond to the letter, and most replied from the perspective of acceptance—"he should find the Quiet beyond all sound," for example. "All good answers," the teacher said. "But, the simplest answer is: Move. Just move. Why do you stay there?"

Once you have cultivated a ground of acceptance, you have the equanimity to hear your voice of wisdom clearly. Reflecting on the practitioner above, acceptance might have nourished wisdom in a reflection such as, "Yes, you can live here. Yes, you can see beauty in this home. Yes you can find quiet beneath the sound. But is this the home that most truly serves your path?"

On a quick path, you start from the perspective of loving awareness, using wisdom to identify the structures, opportunities, and relationships in your life that serve your soul's purpose. This perspective allows you to employ compassion and courage to shape your world to suit your deepest needs. In walking this path, you develop discriminating wisdom—an ability to analyze effectively without being judgmental and, in the context of choosing your path, to be able to see the obstructions and hindrances you would be better off without. It is important to remember that, by streamlining your life, you are not running away from or avoiding aspects of yourself or your life. Rather, you are engaged in a creative process of building a life that most beautifully aligns with your truest "you."

I love Henry David Thoreau's insight in following this path: "If one advances confidently in the direction of his dreams, and endeavors to live the life which he has imagined, he will meet with a success unexpected in common hours." On a quick path, you work towards drawing in the people and opportunities that align with your purpose, as well as supporting others as they grow authentically. On this path, you may frequently ask, *Which choice best serves my soul's purpose?* or *Whom am I here to serve?* This path can teach powerful, life-changing lessons, such as a deepening trust that the universe will support your endeavors and that you will always somehow be profoundly well. Even when things don't go according to plan, your engaged creativity will enable you to see beauty and opportunity in whatever arises. Moreover, you will find that whenever you act in accordance with your purpose, living your life authentically, incredible opportunities will open to you without your consciously having sought them out.

A focus on cultivating favorable life circumstances can create tremendous opportunities and uncover incredible beauty. It is a wonderful approach to life for artists, entrepreneurs, and, truly, anyone who would like to discover and walk his or her authentic path. Such an approach might focus on improving aspects of your personal life, such as enhancing your living situation or finding a compatible partner. Or, it could be more publicly-oriented, focusing on social justice or a career in service to others. Either way, the practice involves visualizing and intuiting a more beautiful reality.

In shaping your world to support your authentic path, you may request support from God, or Spirit, or angels (if doing so resonates with you). In addressing a power beyond yourself, you most likely request as a co-creator or a conduit (rather than as a supplicant). And yet, even as you visualize and intuit more authentic life circumstances, you wisely leave a window open to grace, such as with the phrase, *not my will, but Thine, be done.*

One of the pitfalls associated with a focus on life circumstances is that we can fall into neglecting the inner practice of acceptance. This neglect stunts the growth of the wisdom of equanimity, leading to an insidious buildup of mental and emotional tension. We often feel judgmental of, and dismissive towards, whatever is actually present— whether that takes the form of experiences, other people, or our own personal traits. And, we can feel guilty or accusatory when things don't go as planned.

In addition, when we focus on the life circumstances we feel we need or deserve without also cultivating acceptance for what is present, we may become functionally paralyzed. On the one hand, we may collapse under the pressure of self-doubt if we imagine we don't deserve our path or that we can't live it. On the other hand, we may feel so entitled to our path that we aren't willing to truthfully assess where we are, and the work we need to do to create more beneficial life circumstances. Moreover, when we are focused on our *ideas* of what our life should be, without accepting what is *present*, we can overlook spectacular unexpected opportunities as they arise.

A wonderful thing about being human is that we can choose to accept what is present while simultaneously enlisting our wisdom, exercising our creativity, deepening our compassion, and practicing our free will. By combining acceptance with wisdom and compassion, we can find the Flow while staying engaged and open to shaping deeper possibilities. These different approaches are complementary and synergistic: each works more effectively when the practices are combined in an interactive dance. It is essential to work with focus, to let the creative juices flow, and to live from that place where acceptance meets imagination.

I have developed an appreciation for the beauty of weaving these approaches together with a magical *and*. That is, it's important to be happy wherever you are. Focusing on how things could be, without accepting and meeting life *as it is*, makes it easy to be ungrounded, bitter, and in other ways at least partially closed off from the beauty inherent in the present. *And*, it's important to intuit your highest calling, tapping into your passion and drive, and to walk your path. When you unite acceptance with wisdom and courage, you realize that, even when life doesn't go as you want, you always have the choice to be open to the unexpected opportunities that actually present themselves. You therefore remain able to take advantage of tremendous opportunities for growth—both imagined and unimaginable.

Stepping up to the plate

There are two mistakes along the road to truth…
not going all the way and not starting.
—Buddha—

There is an astounding wealth of information available to us these days—in blogs, in books, in webinars, in direct meetings, and in other ways. Although this information can be truly helpful, the key to processing it is to receive words as signposts and not as answers. Answers that were perfect for one person may not suit another. Each of us has a unique set of challenges, understandings, gifts, and passions. To live authentically, we each have to discover truths for ourselves. Merely knowing our path is not enough; we must actually walk it.

I see *help* as a double-edged sword. On the one hand, it's incredibly useful to share perspectives with each other. I've benefited immeasurably by hearing or reading about other people's journeys—their challenges, responses to challenges, and subsequent successes and discoveries. I've also found that it can be quite valuable to hear other people's insights into my own life, as fresh perspectives can introduce new avenues of discovery and growth. I feel tremendously grateful for the authentic teachers who have shared their wisdom with me, and I truly believe that we can be tremendous blessings to each other when we speak truth with compassion and wisdom. Even so, I've also noticed that the pattern of teaching and helping, when used inappropriately, can become a sort of trap, fostering dependence and numbness rather than freedom, empowerment, and exploration.

It is too easy—even addictive—to seek answers outside yourself, whether from psychoanalysis, workshops, self-help books, tarot readers, or any of the various paths of religion and spirituality. Any of these strategies can be useful; you might encounter skillful techniques and insights that help you align your path to your true purpose in life. But in the end the techniques are no substitute for direct experience. Unless external answers are received as suggestions to guide deeper internal investigations rather than as discoveries in themselves, they are reduced to entertaining diversions at best. At worst, life graciously jolts you awake: life highlights the difference between innate and borrowed wisdom by knocking you down when you reflexively accept others' ideas instead of consciously intuiting your own truths. By learning from these experiences, we deepen in wisdom that sustains us through life's varying circumstances.

The Buddha said, "Better than a thousand hollow words, is one word that brings peace." And yet, unless that one word is treated as a signpost instead of an answer, no real peace can be found. On an authentic path, the essential element is to truly experience heart opening, rather than simply relying on *ideas* of stillness, or *ideas* of safety or trust, repeating aphorisms and such. Words can be beautiful, but they are only useful when they inspire you to truly experience your own limitless depths. In many spiritual paths and psychological disciplines, the central underlying tenet is that one should accept nothing unquestioningly. Every understanding should be truly investigated so that you can find the truth for yourself. The teachings are simply a boat that may be useful in crossing life's rivers. The boat is only useful in so far as it supports the journey.

In Western education, we often believe that it is the teacher's job to ensure that the student learns what he or she needs to know. But in fact we all know that the responsibility for learning is shared. In life, just as in education, a useful guide knows a subject and presents it accessibly. But true learning will not occur until you bring your full attention to the task. You can discover what is true for you only by actively wrestling with the material before you. This sense of shared responsibility is essential in deeper learning and in transformation. As you read through these pages, I invite you to take time for investigation and contemplation. I provide many suggestions for personal exploration. I hope you will delve into these exercises, and also that you will be inspired to follow your creative intuition to dive more deeply into your truth.

NOURISHING THE GROUND

Mindfulness

There are no ordinary moments.
—Dan Millman—

Mindfulness: Noticing what is present

Before we have the opportunity to open to acceptance, it is essential to first notice the thoughts, beliefs, and reactions that zip through our consciousness. We must take a step into mindfulness: becoming aware of whatever is present in our minds, bodies, and hearts. This skill is variously referred to as recognition, mindfulness, or presence. It is most easily described as being consciously aware of whatever is going on *right now*—maintaining calm awareness of your bodily sensations, emotions, and thoughts. I think of mindfulness as a prerequisite for acceptance because we need to honestly recognize what is present before we have the opportunity to consciously accept it.

Healthy animals are really good at registering patterns subconsciously and creating useful habits and routines. In nature, migrating animals return to the sites where they have found food, water, and shelter in the past. When people discover tools that are helpful in completing tasks, they tend to use them again and again in the same ways without giving it much thought. For example, how often do you think about the way to hold your pen? If you're like most of us, it's only when the old way doesn't work, perhaps due to an injury or an attempt to write on an awkward surface.

When I work with people who have had brain injuries, or who have attention deficit challenges, it is easy to see how we make our lives easier by unconsciously developing habits and routines. People who have a limited capacity for habitual organization often perform poorly on repetitive tasks. They find themselves repeatedly *reinventing the wheel* rather than simply following a sequence of steps to complete a project, and they may miss critical steps. On longer projects, they often find themselves scrambling at the last minute because they have not effectively identified steps and assigned milestones to support getting the project done on time. As well, people with brain injuries or attention challenges often have difficulty noticing some details and ignoring others. In busy environments, they may work inefficiently because they are unable to filter out irrelevant sights and sounds.

On the other hand, relying too much on habits and routines can be at least as troublesome. Especially when we have fast-paced work or home environments, it's easy for us to slip into autopilot, zipping through our activities with insufficient awareness to take advantage of opportunities for learning and growth for ourselves or our loved ones. We may get swept into our bodies' stress reactions without even noticing that we have rapid, shallow breathing or tense shoulders, or that we've devoured our dinner in five minutes. We may miss warning signs and find ourselves surprised by unanticipated crises, staying on task as if everything were fine even after circumstances have changed fundamentally. We see this in people who, while experiencing a heart attack or stroke, initially try to keep on with their normal routine, only realizing that they require immediate medical help when their bodies simply cannot function.

For a long while, I had the following quote posted above my desk: *There are no ordinary moments*. When life feels fast-paced or repetitive, it can be especially easy to slip into unconscious patterns. But what if we decide we don't need to be fast? What if we decide that we don't have to do what we've always done? What if we decide that we don't need to do *more*, but rather to live *more consciously*? What if we decide to truly notice every moment?

There are innumerable activities that can invite your mind to slow down and to become more aware of the current moment. Truly, any activity (doing dishes, walking dogs, sipping coffee) performed consciously can become a form of meditation and mindfulness training. Even so, once you look for opportunities, you'll likely notice that certain activities provide more welcoming invitations for you compared to others.

For me, yoga, gardening, and playing with my pets are wonderful ways to slip effortlessly into the present moment. On the other hand, it takes more conscious effort for me to maintain mindfulness while performing such activities as driving or grocery shopping. For my boyfriend, fast-paced activities like mountain biking and snowboarding provide his most accessible occasions for being present; slower-paced activities require more effort for him to perform mindfully. I remember once hearing a talk by a lovely senior Catholic nun. She said that she relished waking 30 minutes early each morning, taking the time to slowly, mindfully sip a cup of tea before her day's activities began. It's useful to notice what works naturally for you, as well as the activities for which mindfulness requires more conscious effort. Both situations provide beautiful opportunities to deepen your experience of life as you live it.

Personal Exploration #2: Noticing your body's experience

One of my favorite mindfulness activities is to tune into my senses as much as possible while engaged on a walk. While it's lovely to explore natural places like rolling hills and quiet beaches, you can have a sensory walk in whatever space life brings you—on a suburban residential street, in a park, or even in your own backyard. If walking is difficult for you, you may find sitting and tuning into your senses gives you a more mindful experience.

We have seven basic senses: sight, hearing, smell, taste, and touch, as well as our internal senses of our body's position and movement. During this exercise, I invite you to truly tune into each of your senses. What do you see? Can you see something you've never noticed before? What do you hear? If there are birds, insects, or frogs chirping, can you distinguish the songs? Can you locate the sources of the calls? Do you hear replies? Do you hear distant dog barks? The swoosh of traffic? Can you sense sweet smells? Pungent smells? Earthy smells? How close must you be to vegetation before you smell its fragrance? Do you have an experience of taste? Can you feel the wind, or coolness, or heat on your skin? Notice how your tactile experience changes as you pass from sunbeam to shadow. If you are walking, notice the feel of your feet as they land on different surfaces. Can you feel the heat or the coolness of the pavement? Do you feel the soft landing of grass or sand? The firmness of asphalt? The stickiness or slickness of mud? Notice how your body registers changes in slope. Can you tune into smaller muscle groups as you move? Can you sense your body's position?

If you are sitting, notice how it feels to sit on your seat. Check in with your body: Are you leaning to one side? Do you have tension in your body? If so, where? Can you release it and find balance and ease?

As you notice your sensory experiences, check in with yourself to acknowledge your natural reactions. As you do, try to let go of as many layers of thought as you can. Let go of any stories, reminiscences, or judgments (including ideas of liking or disliking sensations) about whatever you are experiencing. Simply become aware of your own spontaneous reactions. You may notice a change in breath, in pace, or in sensations in the head, gut, or heart. You may notice an unconscious smile or furrowed brow. You may notice a feeling of wanting to linger or to hurry away. Without ideas about how you *should* react, see what arises naturally. Feel free to deepen this practice using your own creativity as a guide for greater mindfulness of your current moment.

Becoming mindful of the world around you

In developing mindfulness, it can be invaluable to tune your attention towards discovering opportunities to offer simple kindnesses to others. How many moments can you identify and act upon to offer gentleness, support, and help towards others in your life? When you tune in mindfully to those around you, you discover the value of small gestures, kind words, reassuring smiles, and timely information delivered clearly, with loving attention. And as you focus on kindness, notice how you are simultaneously honing your skillfulness at being aware of what is present around you.

Becoming more consciously aware of the natural world can also help us become more mindful. For example, I like to keep the temperature in my house somewhat consistent with the weather (within safety limits for my pets and pipes). So I might keep my house at 60 degrees in the winter and 80 degrees in the summer. I also love the feel of the summer night flooding my home as fans pull in cool breezes. I do appreciate that this arrangement is a luxury in Colorado that isn't available in less temperate climates. Perhaps where you live, you'll find a different way to comfortably invite more of nature's fluctuations into your home. Or perhaps you will feel more conscious of the natural world by eating foods grown in season. If they come from your garden, or from the farmer's market, so much the better! Can you taste the sunshine and the rain as you slowly, consciously experience each bite?

Perhaps you enjoy getting out in nature, visiting a beach, mountain, or neighborhood park. Instead of waiting for a perfect day, with perfect weather, experience the beauty of consciously spending time in nature whether skies are overcast or sunny.

Embracing creativity and play

Creativity means loving whatsoever you do—
enjoying, celebrating it, as a gift of existence!
—Osho—

Some of us are *thinkers*, while others are more *doers*. Perhaps you tend to feel more present when engaged actively in tasks. If so, you may find that creativity provides a beautiful invitation for you to deepen in mindfulness.

Personal Exploration #3:   Exploring creativity

If you feel relaxed and engaged when you are writing or drawing, you may find that keeping a *creativity journal* will enhance your mindfulness practice. You may, for example, choose to take a journal with you as you go for walks or hikes, drawing or writing about what you see as inspiration moves you. I've been surprised at how much I notice, and how present I feel, when I consciously choose to draw an insect or flower, or even the unique, intricate patterns of tree bark. Similarly, lovely ideas and poetry have flowed when I've traveled to a stark, isolated location, committed to simply being quiet and present, writing only when I felt the inspiration.

You may find that creative photography helps you to notice the world around you and to see the world in a new way. Perhaps dancing provides you a doorway into presence. Notice where you feel naturally pulled towards creativity and see if you can use that inspiration to more deeply open to mindful awareness of the world within and around you.

Meditation

Seated meditation is a wonderful practice. It is accessible whenever and wherever you can take a few minutes for undivided attention. Truly meditating for even a minute is beneficial, and the deepening awareness you can access in longer meditations is profoundly rewarding. It can be helpful to choose a set daily time to establish your meditative practice, such as at the beginning or ending of your day. Or, you may choose to meditate in your car for a few minutes before beginning your work day, or as part of your lunch break.

Whenever you are establishing a new habit, it is helpful to set a realistic goal. To create a meditative practice, I recommend committing to 5 or 10 minutes of daily meditation at a set time. As you deepen your meditative practice, you'll likely feel drawn to increase the time you commit to meditation. It is also lovely to meditate whenever inspiration strikes. When you are doing an outdoor task or activity, and you are ready for a break, you may feel naturally drawn to meditate right where you are. It is beautiful to follow those waves of inspiration (except, of course, when engaged in potentially dangerous activities, like driving a car or operating power tools).

There are innumerable variations on the theme of seated meditation, such as focusing on the breath, or a candle's flame, or a sacred symbol, or a sacred chant. While it can be wonderful to add lovely elements to your meditation space, such as candles, incense, or flowers, none of that is required. I have found that the single most important thing in supporting a deeper meditation practice is finding as much attentive ease in the physical body as possible.

Personal Exploration #4:   Finding your meditative seat

Before you begin, I recommend laying the groundwork to give yourself the gift of uninterrupted time for meditation. For example, turn your phone off. Don't just set the ringer to *vibrate*; actually turn the ringer off. If there are others around you who may knock on your door, perhaps consider placing a *Do Not Disturb* sign on your door.

If you can sit comfortably on a meditation cushion, wonderful. If you require a chair with a back for comfort, please find a suitable chair. You can lie down if that's what your body requires to be comfortable. However, note that lying down is the "least best" choice since that posture tends to make it more challenging to focus (and much easier to fall asleep).

To begin, tap into your internal senses to feel your body's position. You may find it easier to feel with your eyes closed. You may find you can elongate your spine by slightly tucking your chin and lifting through the crown of your head. If your shoulders feel rounded, you may find you can open your heart space by rolling your shoulders back and sliding your shoulder blades down your back. If seated, you may gently sway side-to-side, front-to-back, perhaps easy circles each direction as you slowly and mindfully identify your center point of balance. If you have tension in your body, you may find that tensing everything for a moment helps your body to relax.

Sitting or lying down, it may feel most welcome to place your palms facing upward, in a *giving and receiving* pose. Or, you may feel more drawn to face your palms downward, in a *calm abiding* pose. You may find that closing your eyes helps to bring your attention inward. Or you may find that closing your eyes makes it too easy to feel sleepy or spacey—in which case you may find a richer meditative experience with eyes open, softly focused, perhaps attending to the "third eye" (just a little above the midpoint between the eye brows).

Once you have your meditative seat (your posture that supports calm awareness and focused attention), you can explore whatever meditative practice calls to you.

The mind-body connection

My research has shown me that the body can
and must be healed through the mind, and the mind can
and must be healed through the body.
—Candace B. Pert, PhD—

Doctor Candace B. Pert's engaging book, *Molecules of Emotion,* describes her scientific research into peptides (molecules consisting of two or more amino acids, similar to but smaller than proteins) and peptide receptors. A tremendous amount of communication between the brain and other organ systems is mediated by the release of various peptides that bind to specific receptors, thereby triggering a wide range of effects throughout the body.

At the beginning of her career, Pert worked with a research team that discovered the opiate receptors—the receptors that bind to both the body's natural endorphins (pain relievers) as well as opiate drugs (such as morphine and heroin). She later supervised a National Institute of Mental Health (NIMH) laboratory that mapped many different types of peptide receptors throughout the body. What she discovered is that the same types of receptors (that is, receptors for the same sorts of peptides) are found in many areas of the body—in the brain, along the intestines, and on immune system cells. Consequently, when the body is flushed with any given peptide, we experience its effects in the mind, in immediate physical sensations, in the immune system's strength, in the digestive system, and elsewhere.

Pert found parallels between her research and Eastern medicine. She wrote that a yogi came into her NIMH office with a map of the chakras (the seven major energy centers in Eastern medicine that align along the spine and head). When Pert and the yogi compared his map against her receptor mappings, they found the places of densest receptor concentrations aligned well with the locations of chakras.

In Eastern medicine, blockages in each chakra are associated with specific mental and emotional challenges. For chakras 1 through 7 respectively, blockages are associated with feelings of anxiety, stifled creativity, powerlessness, bitterness, self-censorship, self-doubt, and alienation. When chakras 1 through 7 have clear flow, they are associated with feelings of security, creativity, personal power, interconnectedness, clear communication, trust, and joy.

In addition to the mental and emotional effects of blocked chakras, Eastern medicine associates blockages in each chakra with specific physical ailments. In Eastern medicine, addressing the underlying mental and emotional blockages is considered essential in helping to keep the physical body healthy. The reverse is also true; just as redressing mental and emotional imbalances promotes physical health, becoming physically healthy also supports emotional well-being.

In yoga, we talk about locating where in our body we feel constriction or discomfort. This identification is useful because one way to look at discomfort is that its location indicates a place where we are blocked or where we are losing energy. For example, when you are concerned about financial issues, career road blocks, or school exams, you might feel cramping in the belly—near the chakra associated with personal power. When you are grieving, or when you are angry, you might feel it as a constriction in the heart—the chakra associated with love, balance, and acceptance. Many people find that they feel a constriction in the throat when they are disguising their emotions by feigning happiness or silently enduring unsuitable situations. The chakra associated with communication is in the area of the throat.

Yogic philosophy suggests these sensations can eventually develop into pathology. Thus, people who feel perennially anxious and suffer from chronic stomach pain may develop stomach ulcers; the chronically short-tempered or depressed may see their chest tightness progress into a heart attack; and those who suffer in silence may find that the tightness in their throat turns into seized vocal cords or thyroid disease. This is the logic behind the yogic approach of acknowledging discomfort and actively exploring the mechanisms of resistance before they can seriously damage our physical and mental health. Of course, whenever we are suffering from significant physical pain, we should first get medical attention to attempt to diagnose what is happening inside our body. But if, as often happens, our doctor is unable to identify a clear physical cause, yoga invites us to consider a more subtle cause for our discomfort. This is the reason I try to appreciate a cold as a gift: as a relatively benign messenger reminding me that I need to attend to my body's needs, and to restore physical and psychological balance.

As Pert explains, Western medicine still does not fully acknowledge the interconnection between the body and the mind. In the words of Dr. Pert, "My research has shown me that the body can and must be healed through the mind, and the mind can and must be healed through the body." She goes on to say that, while Western medicine's externally-focused recommendations for wellness (including healthy diet, daily exercise, and avoiding toxins) are health-supporting, they would be much more effective if they were combined with an equal concern for emotional self-care, including becoming more aware of our thoughts and feelings. She writes, "the emotions are a key element in self-care because they allow us to enter into the bodymind's conversation. By getting in touch with our emotions, both by listening to them and by directing them through the psychosomatic network, we gain access to the healing wisdom that is everyone's natural biological birthright."

Personal Exploration #5:   Somatic awareness

When you are feeling upset—angry, sad, frustrated, anxious, or any other unbalanced emotion—see if you can bring your awareness into your body and notice where your emotion resides. When you first begin practicing this exercise, you'll probably be more successful in dealing with more subtle emotional imbalances because it is easier to be a non-interfering witness when your emotions are less extreme. Try to let go of your expectations and simply experience how your body carries your emotion before your thinking mind affects the process. Where is your emotion sitting? Do you feel a buzzing in your arms or legs? Do you feel constriction in your chest? Do you feel a headache developing? Do you feel a tightening in your gut? Without trying to will it away, or to exaggerate its sensations, see if you can simply notice where in your body you feel your emotional state.

Once you have found it, sit in witness. Is it constant, or is it shifting? Don't try to change it—either to intensify it or to soften it. Simply witness how your body experiences the emotion. Personally, once I feel that I have been able to witness it, I like to offer gratitude to my body for reflecting my emotional state to me.

A wonderful thing about the body is that, just as our mind and emotions shape our physical experience, our physical experience similarly affects our thoughts and emotions. Notice your posture and your breath. Is your breath quick and shallow? Let's see if you can slow your breath down, creating even in-breaths and out-breaths four seconds or so in length. Perhaps you can slow down your breathing even further.

Place a hand on your belly and a hand on your heart. Notice how your torso naturally fills with air. Is your belly expanding and softening with each in-breath and out-breath? Is your chest rising and falling? If not, see if you can give your lungs more space in every breath by sitting or standing tall and consciously breathing into both chest and belly. As you inhale, your belly expands and your chest rises. As you exhale, your chest falls and your belly squeezes out the last bit of air.

Now, feel your body beyond your breath. Are your shoulders rounded or raised? If so, can you soften them to neutral? Is your body tense? In relaxing, it can be very helpful to first tense everything in your body and then consciously release into ease. Are you leaning to one side or the other? If so, can you find your seat of more effortless balance? You may find physical balance is more easily attained by slowly shifting forward and back, left and right, until you come upon your natural balance. Now, sense again. Can you find a place of unease in your body—a constriction, tension, or other discomfort? If so, can you breathe into that place, inviting it to soften? Breathing in, feel light and love cleansing the unease. Breathing out, let it go.

Once you've at least partially dissolved your body's tension, and you feel yourself in greater physical balance, gently witness once again. What emotion is most present for you now? Can you feel how gently working with your body has softened your emotional state? Perhaps you notice a difference, and perhaps you don't. Know that either experience is okay. We are simply working right now on noticing our experiences—increasing our awareness of the connection between physical and emotional experiences. I've found that the process of witnessing my body's uncomfortable sensations and thanking them for their messages often results in their release. However, whenever I continue to experience discomfort in my body, I might choose to invite its cleansing, using creative intuition to guide the process. I might visualize light blasting through a constriction, or a subtle breeze gently dissolving it. Feel free to tap into your intuition and to follow its guidance as you deepen your somatic awareness. Again, of course, it is important to get medical attention to check out exactly what is happening in your body if you are concerned about sensations, including physical pains or challenges with breathing.

The monkey mind

Sometimes, when I sit down to meditate, there are a thousand thoughts whizzing through my mind. If the thoughts have practical content (like things I need to do), it is often useful to simply jot them down in a list and then to tell myself those thoughts can be released, as they are duly noted. Sometimes, I make two lists (such as things I must do at work, and items I must pick up on the way home). Once something is on a list, if it enters my thoughts again, I simply tell it "No… you are on the list. Be quiet." Somehow, that trick works really well for me, and I am able to meditate more efficiently and single-mindedly.

There are, however, at times, swirling thoughts that I simply won't immediately be able to do anything about, such as worries, regrets, fears, or plans for the future. Some people call this active mental chatter (the confused, restless and uncontrollable thoughts whizzing by) the experience of the *monkey mind*. As much as my mind might want to process its seemingly limitless notions, I also know my monkey mind always finds more to ponder. So, it is useless to wait to meditate until all those ideas get processed. Instead, I've found that a clearing meditation can be a very useful way to quiet the mind in the first few minutes of my meditation before I dive more deeply inward.

Personal Exploration #6:   Meditation for mental clarity

First, find your meditative seat following the basic steps described in *Personal Exploration #4: Finding your meditative seat*. With your balanced, aware seat, visualize roots extending from your base into the earth. Visualize your chaotic thoughts flowing down your roots and dissolving into magma. While maintaining the visualization of roots, visualize a golden egg around you, extending perhaps two feet beyond your body in each direction. Visualize golden or pink light flowing downward through the crown of your head, cleansing your body, mind, and spirit, and filling you and the egg surrounding you with its light.

Maintaining this visualization, add breath and meditative words. Inhaling slowly, visualize light flowing into your crown while you mentally verbalize "let." Exhaling slowly, and visualizing mental chatter flowing out through your roots and dissolving in the earth's core, mentally verbalize "go." Continue this meditation until you feel mental clarity. Once you do, envision dissolving your roots and sealing your crown. I find offering gratitude and meditating on my heart chakra (the center of love and balance) is a beautiful way to seal this practice.

Acceptance and Gratitude

Just play. Have fun. Enjoy the game.
—Michael Jordan—

Leela's dance

Leela is an exquisite concept celebrated in Hindu philosophy. It's sometimes translated as "divine play," and it implies freedom and spontaneity (in contrast with conscious effort or necessity). The freedom of Leela welcomes whatever arises, and sees beauty in whatever appears. The joy of Leela is often compared to watching competitive sports. In sports, the focused intent of the players, the possibility of failure, and the unpredictability of the outcome all add to the joy in watching a game. Similarly, the excitement of Leela builds with each of these elements.

Leela's playful essence welcomes pain as well as joy, struggle as well as success, and it transcends it all. Discovering Leela can bring a welcome laugh in times of disruption. Just when you've put forth your best efforts and yet everything seems wrong, just when nothing is going according to plan, you feel the divine bliss of a shrug that says, "Yes! This is so *not* what I expected!"

Most of us have pretty set ideas about how things will work out, or about how things should be. We work on a physical level, putting ourselves through school, arduously developing our careers, consciously raising our children, typically with specific goals and plans in mind. We work on ourselves mentally and emotionally, often with careful checklists about how we should and should not be. Goals and plans are beautiful—and having a sense of direction in life is valuable. And yet, sometimes, that trickster Chance, or Unintended Consequences, sneaks in, shakes up the whole field of play, and leaves with a merry dance. The puzzle the Trickster asks us to unravel is, *Can you find the bliss?*

As much fun as it is to set and meet goals, it can be so beautiful to completely miss, fumble the ball, and discover in that slip the joyful feel of open hands and the incredible smell of freshly mown grass inches from your nose.

Personal Exploration #7:   Experiencing the joy of Leela

I'm sure that everyone has experienced life spiraling away from expectations. Perhaps you've reacted to those sorts of situations with some sort of resistance—denial, or blame, or fury, for example. If so, maybe you noticed that your resistance added to your discomfort. Perhaps you discovered that, when you let go of that desire to control, and chose instead to rest in the beauty of life *as it is*, you were able to find deepening peace. By recognizing and working with life's flow, by swimming without struggling, we find that we are life's dance, and that within its movement is an exquisite stillness.

Misadventures are beautiful to contemplate in their own right. Can you find the joy in contemplating aspects of your life that aren't going quite as you had hoped? In this contemplation, don't focus on how you can fix your circumstances; rather, listen for the gifts they offer. Quite wonderfully, when you let go of your ideas about how things *should* be, it is interesting to see what inherent beauty becomes obvious. See what arises for you when you are willing to meet your life with calm, interested witnessing. See if you can discover the tremendous freedom and ease that appear when you let go of your expectations and desires and choose instead presence and welcome.

The nature of suffering

*A warrior cannot complain or regret anything. His life
is an endless challenge, and challenges cannot possibly
be good or bad. Challenges are simply challenges.*
—Carlos Castaneda—

It's natural for us to think that our suffering is caused by unpleasant or undesirable circumstances. And yet, when we truly study the nature of suffering, we see that its roots are actually our desires and aversions—our wanting things to be different from how they are. By not accepting our personal qualities or life situations, we create a lot of suffering for ourselves and for those around us. Thankfully, we can change our mental patterns by developing skillful acceptance. We can sand away those thought processes that support the illusion that we must suffer if things don't work out as we imagine they should. In fact, we can go one step further, letting go of the imagining entirely so that we can meet life directly, just as it is.

Both Buddhism and Taoism ask us to question the belief that we will be happy only if we get what we want. Both philosophies suggest that, when we honestly examine our experiences, we find that either (a) we get what we want and we suffer because it's not that great or we fear we'll lose it, —*or*— (b) we don't get what we want (or we get what we don't want) and we suffer because our thoughts blind us to the grace in what is inherently present. One insight that both Taoists and Buddhists explore is that, through *acceptance* (that is, by letting go of the idea that life has to be one particular way), we can, ironically, be truly and deeply happy, and we can live a life of joyful authenticity.

In life, of course, we experience a wide range of events—painful, melancholic, ecstatic—and everything in between. From the perspective of acceptance, events are not unavoidable causes of suffering. Rather, events are simply events. Suffering arises from our mental activity, our response to whatever is present, such as longing for what isn't or pushing away what is. When circumstances are joyful, we may suffer from thinking about times before they occurred or after they will end. When circumstances are painful, we may suffer by blaming ourselves for them, feeling resentment towards others, or imagining situations will never change—or that they will get progressively worse. We suffer when we resist life instead of accepting that situations and people are simply however they are.

At times, there is enjoyment in suffering itself. For example, you might feel happy with events or people in your life and yet simultaneously experience the melancholy associated with knowing that they can't last. Or, in less pleasurable events, you may enjoy the bitter sweetness inherent in longing and nostalgia, the escapist delight in clinging to false hopes, even the self-righteous fervor of feeling wronged. In fact, sometimes, the pleasure inherent in suffering can make it difficult to delve into its mechanisms. In truth, we actually enjoy clinging to our illusions, and we imagine that reality will not compare favorably to our ideas of how things should be. The good news is that, truly, our thought patterns are worth studying.

We tend to be such creatures of habit that, when you begin to study your patterns, you will likely need to focus your attention to notice where you suffer. When you pay attention, you might experience suffering as excessive mental activity… as racing thoughts that block your ability to focus or to open to love. You might notice vague feelings of friction, pressure, or discomfort or more specific emotions like fear, shame, blame, guilt, resentment or anger. A fortunate aspect of suffering is that, because it is a mental activity, it becomes much more obviously a choice as you grow more conscious. Moreover, it reliably points directly at whatever it is that you most resist about your current reality.

It is natural to want to chase after love, or peace, or stillness, or bliss, but those states cannot be captured. Rather, those states are our natural states, beneath our mental activity. Our suffering is quite simply our own creation, a product of an over-thinking mind. By letting go of our concepts and expectations of how things *should* be, we create the opportunity to discover the beauty inherent in how things truly are. We clear away excess mental activity in order to feel our natural state of luminous awareness.

Sounds straightforward enough, right? And yet, struggling against our thoughts—or reasoning with them, or believing them—won't help with the clearing. As counterintuitive as it may seem, we need to *rest* in the *discomfort*, to give the suffering itself the loving awareness that shines it into meaning and makes its message sing. By resting in the question, *what most needs to heal?* and by providing our thoughts with sacred space to exist without indulging them, we can directly experience the gifts our suffering provides.

Personal Exploration #8:   Recognition and allowing

Of course, we all have ideas of what life should be. Part of being alive is having ideas. The key, from my perspective, lies in not taking our ideas too seriously. When I let go of my own ideas of who I am, or how the world should be, I create space to allow myself to center on Love (or Eternity, Source, Goddess, or whatever speaks most closely to your heart).

Certain thoughts make it especially hard to hear the whispers of intuition. When our thoughts swirl with emotions that we haven't fully processed (such as fear, resentment, shame, or guilt), or when we have a loud inner critic, it can be especially difficult to trust our intuition. Moreover, feeling unsure of our how we'll meet our basic survival needs (food, shelter, and connection) can also make it especially difficult to tap into our authentic path. It is easiest to quiet the thinking mind with a practice of mindfulness if we first recognize whatever thoughts are arising, and then simply sit in awareness of the thoughts. Don't try to follow the thoughts or suppress the thoughts, and don't reason with the thoughts or pacify the thoughts. Instead, simply shine love inward, providing recognition and awareness for the thoughts. Gradually, you will discover they soften and dissolve. The space they leave behind gives room for intuitive knowing to take root and grow.

Self acceptance

One of the central tenets in many self-help books is that we must love ourselves before we can love others, or even receive their love. I remember talking once with a very dear, practical friend who said something like, "yeah, but what if you're an a**hole?" I laughed out loud, both because of the blunt non-political correctness of the question, and also because he got at the crux of the issue for a lot of us. We all have things that we like about ourselves as well as edges that we are working on, places where we act out of habitual patterns, resist life as it is, create disharmony and other sorts of pain for ourselves and for others. We all, at least occasionally, act out of ignorance or "sin"—different philosophies use different terms to describe the same basic struggle.

When we love others, we open our hearts to their eccentricities, and we accept that they have areas in which they are growing. You can ask any parent (or pet guardian, for that matter) if their love is contingent on their loved one's being *perfect*. You'll probably hear a guffaw in response, as well as some funny story about the way the cat wakes them up at 5 o'clock sharp every morning for breakfast, or the time the child used some colorful language in front of the in-laws, or the way their spouse is forever looking for the glasses that sit on the top of their head, or the way their beloved 100-pound dog hides behind the toilet until thunderstorms pass. The same goes, of course, for parents, siblings, friends—and, if we choose, for ourselves, as well.

But, when we consider loving ourselves, our toughest critics often emerge. We may come to believe that, to love ourselves, we have to be *perfect*. Not "we are all, in our essence, expressions of the same Oneness of Light" perfect, but infallibly perfect. Of course, that's silly when it's stated outright. But when it comes to self-love, somehow, it seems far too easy to sit at one or both poles, being alternatively too harsh (criticizing yourself for eccentricities that would be funny in someone you love, or beating yourself up for issues you are working through) or too lenient (pretending that you don't have shortcomings, often by blaming others for *pushing your buttons*).

The key element to this idea of loving yourself is a magical *and* used in the service of truth. That is, we can love ourselves as we are *and* notice when we are out of balance. In fact, that's the best way *to* love yourself. If you had a splinter in your hand, you could ignore it, wait for your body to build up an immune reaction with the accompanying swelling and pain; or you could acknowledge it, remove the splinter, and support your skin's healing. Why pretend the splinter isn't there, allowing it to become a significant, painful infection, possibly with even more serious consequences?

We often treat our physical ailments more sensibly than we do our emotional ailments, but that is our *choice*. We can love ourselves as we are *and* appraise ourselves honestly—distinguishing, for example, between harmless eccentricities and the indulgence of habitual patterns that create disharmony for ourselves and others. We can love ourselves *and* be aware that when someone pushes our buttons, we are seeing our own reflection. And, we can receive that reflection as a gift to support deeper self-discovery.

By loving ourselves with this sort of open acceptance, an acceptance that welcomes *what is* while simultaneously creating opportunities for unfolding wisdom and compassion, we uncover the type of love that all those self-help books are trying to describe. This is a love that makes space for ourselves and everyone we encounter both to be as we are *and* to deepen in peace, understanding, and unconditional love.

The power of gratitude

Gratitude unlocks the fullness of life. It turns what we have into enough, and more. It turns denial into acceptance, chaos to order, confusion to clarity. It can turn a meal into a feast, a house into a home, a stranger into a friend.
—*Melody Beattie*—

Many years ago, I was a college student barely making ends meet. I stayed in California while nearly everyone I knew went home for Thanksgiving. And so, I planned a lovely, solitary celebration of gratitude with things I appreciated, including macaroni and cheese and a long hike through the Berkeley hills. I heard from someone recently that this area is now really crowded. But, at the time, it was pretty sparsely populated; I saw more deer than people on my hike. As I hiked, I had a walking meditation on gratitude, and thanked plants, butterflies, clouds, and deer as they drew my eye.

As I left the hills, a car slowly pulled up beside me, triggering my city instincts. My wary, polite mask emerged effortlessly. But as I looked at the driver's eyes, I relaxed, feeling that she was a sister. She rolled down her window, offered me a ten dollar bill, and wished me a happy Thanksgiving. I was confused at first, and then I remembered that a lot of homeless people lived in the hills, and I looked threadbare enough to be mistaken for one of them. It occurred to me that the lady in the car could be feeling the same gratitude that was washing through me as she gazed at a solitary girl in well-worn clothing, feeling grateful for what she had, knowing others had less. The love and gratitude for her, for having enough, for love itself, poured through my dissolving walls of separation. I laughed, thanked her, and, without taking the cash, said that, really, things were quite okay. And I knew that, truly, they were.

Gratitude is the sincerest form of acceptance. When we accept what life offers, when we accept our own gifts and shortcomings with joy, we find that we truly have infinite opportunities to experience the blessing of deep gratitude.

Personal Exploration #9:   Gratitude

I've found that one of the most powerful ways to shift energy is to make a conscious practice of noticing and acknowledging people, circumstances, and events for which I am grateful. Just after awakening, when you are lying in bed and stretching, consciously reflect on the people and creatures in your life for whom you are grateful. Or, relish some bit of joy you anticipate in your upcoming day, such as the roasty warmth of the coffee you will soon drink, the silkiness of your favorite scarf, or the exhilaration of your early morning workout. Creatively reflect to discover sources of inspiration for gratitude that are meaningful for you. Similarly, before you fall asleep, reflect on your day and consciously express gratitude for particular moments, people, animals, and aspects of yourself, and for the learning opportunities that arose over the course of the day.

When you notice a beautiful moment, such as opening a book to a passage that is *just right*, or seeing an exquisite dance between squirrels, take a moment to appreciate the circumstances. It is wonderful to make a habit of gratitude, whether in the transitions into and out of sleep, or at scheduled times, or simply as inspired throughout the day. Gratitude is especially helpful for maintaining a healthy state of mind when you're feeling stretched a little thin, whether financially, emotionally, or in some other way. There is such beauty and relief in discovering that, even when you worry about whether there is "enough," you are actually lovingly supported throughout your life.

DEVELOPING WISDOM
AND COMPASSION

The Root of Wisdom

There is a voice that doesn't use words. Listen.
—Rumi—

Life's purpose

It seems like everyone has ideas about what *the* purpose of
life is. For some, it's growing rich or well educated. For others,
working hard or "doing good." For still others, it's raising children or
achieving fame. And, for others, it's creating exquisite art or achieving
Enlightenment. Most of us have a lot of conscious and unconscious
ideas about life's purpose, as well as ideas about what a life should
look like. Some of these ideas have been instilled in us from an early
age by parents and movies. Some have developed over time, as we
learned from friends and peers. And we've developed some ourselves
in response to our experiences. We have so many *ideas* that it is useful
to quiet the mind and use the heart to *feel* our authentic purpose
rather than *think* it.

Your authentic path

There is a word in Buddhism that I love for its multifaceted
depths: *Dharma*. Dharma is often translated as *truth*, but it means so
much more. It includes living an authentic life, fulfilling your highest
calling, whether in business, interactions with loved ones, or in your
own path toward self-discovery. Dharma includes honest reflection and
the pursuit of mental clarity, consciously steering your development

toward the "best you," and walking your unique path courageously. Instead of accepting a life that is "good enough," Dharma invites you to look deeper, and to live with more discipline as you orient each moment to your highest calling. Dharma means performing your duties with *right intent*, conducting yourself in alignment with truth in every relationship whether long-lasting or fleeting, and in all spheres of your life, including career, family, and community. In a nutshell, Dharma is about you being your truest, most beautiful, you; opening doors of compassion, truth, and wisdom as you flow through your life.

Painful thoughts and expansive thoughts

> *The trick is in what one emphasizes. We either make*
> *ourselves miserable, or we make ourselves happy.*
> *The amount of work is the same.*
> *—Carlos Castaneda—*

Our minds are naturally systematic. We habitually ruminate on events, fitting them into larger patterns of thinking. This process of integrating and making sense of the world can be beneficial for us. At times, we establish viewpoints that support our sense of trust, love, and ease in the world, and in ourselves. These perspectives support growth, mindfulness, and compassionate living, as well as happiness. However, this process of integration can also create and reinforce painful beliefs that urge us to view the world, others, and ourselves through fearful eyes. We may, for example, ruminate on stories to justify our uncomfortable states of mind, or to beat ourselves up about them. We might pin unflattering labels like *quitter, hot-headed,* or *selfish* on ourselves or loved ones, and we might project our fearfulness on a world that we come to see as unforgiving, untrustworthy, and hostile. The key is to become consciously aware of our recurring thoughts, and to analyze them: feeling around for the ones with heavy emotional content and questioning their validity.

Our world views are rooted in childhood, and we continue to feed and adapt these habits of mind as we integrate new experiences. Typically, we fit events into our frameworks without our even thinking about it. For example, if someone unexpectedly cuts us off in traffic, most of us will automatically feel tension in our bodies and a quick release of adrenalin, which elicits rapid breathing, sweating, and a quickened heart rate. However, the next step—the mental activity that fits the event into a world view—shows that our interpretation of events depends largely on our habits of mind. Does the story of this event corroborate an underlying belief that people are self-absorbed? Foolish? Stupid? Out to get you? Does this near accident become the event that ruined your day? Or does it reinforce gratitude for a near miss? Do you feel compassion for the person who is driving mindlessly, sending them wishes to get where they're going safely? Does this story stick in your mind, which continues to churn with adrenalin-fueled recrimination, or can you let it go?

Each of us has subconscious thoughts, or residues from past experiences, that color our lives, shape our nature, guide our spontaneous responses, and limit our states of mind. Compared to an internal reflection, it's usually a lot easier for us to see these subconscious patterns when we observe them in others. But with disciplined attention, we can also see them when they arise in our own mind. The wonderful news is that we can consciously develop *new* mental habits. We can deepen the wisdom that lets us assess a situation, get out of danger, and let go of the habit of creating and holding onto stories that strengthen painful states of mind.

Our current mental states can be thought of as products of prior mental states. But thankfully, we don't have to live unconsciously, blindly rolling in well-worn mental ruts. By watching our thoughts vigilantly, and by consciously choosing new states of mind, we can deliberately change our mental grooves. We can break through the familiar patterns that no longer serve us in finding love, joy, and peace.

Personal Exploration #10:   Awakening to your habits of mind

Many of us have negative thoughts that don't register in our conscious minds. We are so used to our mind's chatter that we tune it out, even though we still unconsciously absorb and react to the subconscious message. Our spouses, children, and close friends are often much more aware of our painful mental habits than we are. But we can begin to get a better understanding of the nature of our own interior dialogue by making use of the technique of *stream of consciousness* writing.

For this exercise, choose a time of day in which you will have time to write for a few minutes. Don't worry about finding an expensive journal; any pad of paper or spiral notepad will do. If typing is more natural for you, then type. Before you begin, turn off any distractions, such as your cell phone, email, or television. Then, simply write down whatever passes through your mind. Do your best to avoid filtering; this isn't the time for wordsmithing. Simply write out, as honestly as you can, the thoughts you are thinking.

After a few days, or perhaps a week, take a look at your writings. The key in this review is to maintain a spirit of equanimity. You'll want to maintain a non-judgmental, inquisitive study of your thoughts with the gentle acceptance embodied in the acknowledgment, "that's interesting." Do you see any recurring themes? Do you see reflections of habits of mind? You might see some lovely habits—accounts of perseverance, kindness, patience, and wisdom. If so, wonderful! Are you jolted to see mental habits that are less than flattering or clearly counterproductive? If so, don't be dismayed; this is good news, too! You are now aware of habits that were previously hidden, and this insight gives you the opportunity to ditch mental dead weight. Over time, if you attentively witness your thoughts, you will develop the skill to notice your painful thoughts as they arise and uproot them before they establish themselves as mental habits.

Discernment and judgment

One of the most essential aspects for reflection is to learn to recognize the difference between your own processes of *discernment*, which are rooted in acceptance and guided by love-filled curiosity, compared to those of being *judgmental*, which are rooted in fear and guided by stories of need and lack. With *discernment*, you truthfully and dispassionately analyze and appraise a situation. When you are *judgmental*, you qualify that appraisal with heated notions of *good* and *bad*.

It's important to understand that you may *feel* fear when you recognize long-standing habits and patterns that no longer serve you, and you *discern* that it is time for change. It is natural to feel anxious or uneasy when you are preparing to break out of an old, familiar mold into something unfamiliar, even if clearly more powerful and authentic. There is, however, a big difference between the nervousness that arises when we are readying ourselves to take the next step on an authentic path, compared to the visceral *fight-or-flight* messages associated with judgments rooted in fear.

Unlike the mental process of discernment, the process of being *judgmental* is shaped by a false sense of threat. Being judgmental inevitably ends in antipathy towards others, and this antipathy frequently turns inward. When we judge others negatively, we build walls separating us from love, connection, and our authentic path. The faculty of discernment, of perceiving whatever is present without judging it, is filled with loving attention. It welcomes everything, while simultaneously opening to the next perfect step towards deeper truth and joy. Wisdom and authentic living are impossible without discernment.

When we are focused on what we want our world to look like, whether in terms of career, personal success, or broad, societal conditions, it is easy to slip into judgment and condemnation; reality never coincides with our ideals. And, this attitude has serious drawbacks. When we are judgmental, we step outside the flow of life as it is happening, and we superimpose our ideas of what *should be* over whatever actually *is* present. This perspective makes it easy to overlook opportunities that don't match our expectations, and it is a natural ground in which new mental habits of guilt, blame, and resentment take root. Moreover, by investing time and energy in our painful stories, we have less to invest in personal and spiritual growth. It is far more helpful to infuse our acceptance of our current circumstances with a balanced analysis of where we are, where we would like to be, and what it will take to get there.

In effective mindfulness and meditation, self-observation and assessment are critically important. There is, however, no benefit to being judgmental of yourself or others. Focusing on how good or bad you are, or how much better or worse you are than other people, or how *they* are doing it wrong, takes you out of the moment and slows your own development. This is not to say that there is not a need for a teacher to give us corrective feedback, or for you to share insights with a friend on the path. However, understandings are most effectively communicated when they are heart-based, loving, and non-judgmental. This principle of discerning refinement is invaluable on an authentic path. It is with this conscious, compassionate practice that we learn and grow.

Judging and the limitless states of mind

In the development of acceptance and wisdom it is helpful to recognize that there are limitless states of mind, and that each of us has access to only a small subset of those states of mind. A funny moment that taught me about the idiosyncrasy of states of mind occurred during a walk with my dear dog soon after I had adopted him as a puppy. We were out walking in New York City, a place with vast and varied sights, sounds, and especially odors. Somehow, on that day, he found something on a light post so amazing that he kept sniffing, looking at me, sniffing, and looking at me as if to say, "Oh my! You have, I mean *have*, to smell this!" I laughed out loud at the absurdity of the situation, knowing that my nose could not begin to sense whatever he was smelling. Of course, there was also the matter of distinctly different olfactory preferences; he was once annoyed at me for giving him a bath immediately after he found an exquisite dead bird in which to roll. I felt a wave of deep appreciation for him in that moment, and I shared his joy even though I couldn't share his experience.

You may have had a similar experience with a loved one. But if not, you can probably sense the range of available states of mind by reflecting on the mind states you commonly experienced as a child, a teenager, a young adult, and so on. You may discover a consistent trajectory, but you likely will also see that certain emotional states were accessible at one life stage and not another. When I was a teenager, I remember getting easily irritated with small inconveniences. I remember what it felt like to feel frustrated and unsettled, but I don't have direct access to those exact emotions today. Instead, when I feel frustrated now, the feeling is tempered with the gentleness of possibility. When we compare the available states of mind between two people, the differences can be much more extreme. One person's sadness may be far more intense than the most extreme sadness another person has experienced or perhaps, can conceive.

As much as we think we understand what other people are thinking and feeling, there are actually tremendous differences in terms of the states of mind that are available to each of us at a given time. While this realization may sound like it could increase the separation between people, I've found that it actually serves to awaken or deepen compassion. Truly, you can never know exactly where another person is emotionally. Choices that others make that seem irrational to you may be the most reasonable to them within their available states of mind. So, to judge others makes little sense. It makes far more sense to send love and warm wishes, to offer help when doing so is welcome, and to give others the space to grow in their own time and in their own way. Of course, societies do need structures in place to limit this freedom to some extent for the common good. But as individuals, there is no practical reason to judge others. As many mystics have recommended in one way or another over the ages, *Remove the plank from your own eye before you worry about the speck in your neighbor's eye.*

Egotism and humility

Egotism and humility are both loaded terms. Most of us have unspoken ideas about what they mean, and our ideas are often pretty negative. Even so, there is a deep utility in studying these concepts, and a value in investigating them consciously. When I reflect on egotism, I see it as sitting at two poles of being. There is a kind of egotism that leads you to think that you are better than everyone else (more accomplished, more deserving, more brilliant), and a kind that leads you to think that you are worse than everyone else (more sinful, more boring, more unlovable). The specific attributes that we apply to our *more* lists vary, but the sense is the same: I am somehow *more* (or *less*) than anyone else. Most of us struggle between these poles, and most of us spend more time on one end than the other.

People often think of humility as the second pole of egotism, as low self-esteem or a groveling manner. In my view, humility is something vastly more beautiful and essential. Humility is the recognition that, in anything you do, there is probably someone somewhere who does it better, and someone who does it worse. It is recognition that you deserve love and kindness no *more* than anyone else—and, equally essentially, no *less*. A humble person sees beauty in curiosity, in welcoming, and in witnessing life's unfolding. Humility suggests we can shine our light brightly, without fear. Humility suggests that we can invite beauty to flow through us, without feeling like we have to be (or even *could* be) in control. Humility is recognition that there are mysteries in this universe that we haven't solved, and that our mind's activities most likely can never solve.

The egotist believes that life is a zero sum game, that we must struggle and compete for resources, and that for every winner there must also be a loser. This belief feeds into the idea that life is intrinsically competitive rather than an opportunity for exploration, transformation, and growth. It also makes another person's strength, happiness, or power feel threatening. Humility discovers that love, strength, and wisdom are blessings that we all can share, that they are not limited to the few. And, a humble person knows that his joy is not *limited*, but rather *enhanced*, by another's joy.

Some people talk about egotism and humility with different words. The voice of egotism may, for instance, be referred to as the small self, or the egoic self. For some people it is the voice of the thinking mind. The voice of humility may be referred to as the higher self, or the soul's (or, spirit's) voice. Or it may be the voice of the heart. The essential point is not the language, but rather the understanding of these two very different perspectives. To develop wisdom, it is indispensable to shift from ego-led judgment to humble, heart-driven discernment.

Many have noted that, when our ego and spirit are aligned, what we want *is* what serves us. When we are genuinely guided by wisdom and unconditional love, our desires *are* aligned with our path. And yet, we can create a lot of suffering if we assume we are acting from discernment when in fact we are operating from judgment. We can create pain for ourselves by chasing every desire or fleeing every aversion. We might even come to imagine that all that activity is really getting us somewhere. When we become aware of that feeling of unproductive busy-ness, our voice of humility has piped in. We've received a wonderful invitation to reflect on the differing voices in our mind, and a blessed opportunity to tap into our own beautifully humble, discerning wisdom.

Hiding and shining

When it comes to assertive behaviors, many of us were, from an early age, given subtle and not-so-subtle cues about the importance of hiding at least a little: not looking too smart, or too ambitious, or too strong. The cues can be as subtle as loved ones pulling away when we say something penetrating, or they can be as obvious as taunts in school after we've demonstrated that we know the subject matter thoroughly. Many of us were also exposed to the expectation that we should bury our vulnerable emotions. We are allowed to display anger, but we should hide sadness or fear. Many of us were told crying shows weakness.

In adulthood, we often continue our grade school patterns of hiding. When women say something meaningful, we often pull back a bit, hide just a little, so as to be perceived non-threatening (maybe raising the pitch of the voice to sound a little less sure, maybe playing with our hair, maybe offering qualifying remarks to create the impression of hesitancy or doubt, maybe even changing the subject entirely). Men also have mechanisms for hiding. When men feel especially lovingly towards each other, they might mask that softness with more aggressive gestures, like howls, or *chest bumps*, or playful punches. When they feel despondent, they may make grand displays of anger (throwing furniture or punching walls) rather than honestly experiencing and communicating the sadness underlying the fury.

Depending on the circumstances of your upbringing, you might have heard different messages about which authentic aspects of yourself you need to hide, although such messages were more emphatic for some of us. The good news is that, by investigating this tendency to think that we need to hide aspects of ourselves, we create a wonderful tool for self-discovery. One question I like to explore when I notice any of my numerous hiding mechanisms is, *Who feels the need to hide?*

What this investigation reveals for me is that, when we speak and act from truth (from love), when we express the strength, courage, and intimacy that arise from *power to* rather than *power over*, the words release a tremendous amount of potentially transformative energy. And our egoic self, the small *me* that believes that it's fragile, subject to the elements, and limited by circumstances, feels afraid.

In a way, the ego would rather believe that life is oppressive, difficult, a series of incomprehensible struggles, rather than acknowledge that we each choose our lives' parameters to some degree, and that happiness and peace are often the result of our own choices. By hiding, we tacitly acquiesce to the ego's notions of what it needs to be "safe." We hide our power, and we hide our love, in order to make another ego feel more comfortable with whatever power it imagines it has. This practice serves no one, and it stifles the creative fires that fuel authentic living.

We are much more than the ego. There is a deeper self, a well of humble strength that welcomes the challenge of being able to shape its reality, even as the ego cowers in the face of such responsibility. Too often we recoil at the prospect of freedom, drawing back and failing to realize that our deeper, more essential self needs love, light, and transformation as much as the body needs food and water. This deeper self blossoms with honest, unapologetically loving communication.

So we can choose to shine, and to shine in a way that welcomes everyone. By expressing genuine respect, love, and empathy for each other, we welcome the egoic parts of each person to the party our deeper selves are already enjoying. We meet in a celebration of knowing that *our* joy does not reduce *anyone else's* joy, and that our truth and discoveries *add to* everyone's truth and everyone's discoveries. Perhaps some people really aren't ready to acknowledge that we can all shine in love and light together, each flame adding to the others. Even so, I believe that there is a deeper part of each of us that understands this basic principle, that knows that extending love authentically and openly awakens and inspires the deeper self in everyone we touch.

Personal Exploration #11: *Reflection to distinguish voices*

Bring conscious attention to the quiet, insistent voice in your mind. What recurring thoughts do you notice? Do you notice that you frequently compare yourself to others? Perhaps ranking yourself according to personal qualities, talents, possessions, or accomplishments, comparing yourself to loved ones, community members, or celebrities? If it is difficult to slow down your thoughts enough to witness them, you may find it useful to try *Personal Exploration #10: Awakening to your habits of mind* first in order become more aware of your habitual thoughts.

When you notice painful, judgmental thoughts, there is no need to feel badly about them, or to argue with them. Instead, be grateful that you have recognized them. Choose just one thought that has emotional weight for you, something like, *I am too fat*, or *nobody treats me well*, or *I'll never be happy*.

Now endow that thought with loving awareness. I find that it is helpful to meditate on my heart space and to witness with the gentle interest of an impartial observer. For me, one visual that works wonderfully is to think of Captain Jack Sparrow from the movie, *Pirates of the Caribbean*. Regardless of the horrors he saw, he kept his wits and composure, musing simply, "That's interesting..."

As you make space for your painful thoughts, don't struggle against them, or try to polish them, or will them away. Instead, simply witness them. If a painful thought's hold on your mind gently dissolves, wonderful. Often, the simple act of recognizing thoughts dissolves their power. If not, that's good, too. In that case, we'll study it more closely.

Reflect for a moment…Can you think of an instance in which this thought wasn't true? Can you see the issue from an alternative perspective? For example, if your thought is *nobody treats me well*, I'll bet you can remember a past kindness. Again, don't wrestle with the thought. Instead, simply turn it around in your mind's eye, like a jeweler studying an uncut gem, looking for a different perspective. This jeweler's view is the attitude of humility, appreciating that the world is more beautiful, loving, and mysterious than we could ever imagine. If you'd like to study this sort of reflection more deeply, I'd encourage you to look into *The Work*, by Byron Katie, as I find her explorations tremendously accessible and beneficial.

Embracing the Shadows

What if you could open to that frustration,
just for a moment, to discover not just
where love is free flowing... but where it's not?
That is how we all begin to uncover the soft spot within.
—Pema Chödrön—

Welcoming pain as a messenger

The wound is the place where the Light enters you.
—Rumi—

We are learning more and more about the value of using pain as a guide in self-discovery. Pain gives us an unmistakable indication of where we are grasping at or rejecting whatever life is offering. Of course, things come up in life that we may need to change or accept. However, when we face our life with eyes wide open, seeing what is mutable and what is fixed and acting accordingly, we don't suffer. Pain arises when we believe that things should be somehow different from the way they are, and that peace and happiness will elude us until the world, or others, or aspects of ourselves, are transformed. When thoughts arise that things must change for us to feel content, we can choose to become a witness, simply recognizing those painful thoughts and making them our allies. Such thoughts can become our allies if we can use them to become aware of where we step out of the present and into the past (by wallowing in feelings of regret or guilt) or the future (by obsessing with worries or with Utopian ideas of how things *should* be).

It's natural for us to pull away from painful situations. As biological creatures, we are well served by avoiding pain, because pain is often the signal of bodily damage. But when I reflect on the response that is often most beneficial, I find that, rather than pulling away, it is usually far more helpful to identify the root cause of my pain, and to work from that knowledge. On a physical level, I've occasionally ignored pain, only to find that the hotspot on my heel opened into a blister, or the slight irritation in my joint worsened into a limp until I gave it proper attention. Ignoring the pain wasn't helpful, but choosing to be sedentary to avoid it wouldn't have been beneficial, either. The most skillful response was to study the source and to make the necessary adjustments in activity or equipment to facilitate healing.

Noticing emotional pain is just as important, because identifying and working with emotional pain creates tremendous opportunities for spiritual growth. Emotional pain indicates where you most need light, love, and healing. Pain is your friend, directing you right to what you most need to explore. Pain highlights your edge for growth. You might find that you place thoughts that you resist into the shadows of your mind, catching glimpses but averting your eyes from a direct gaze. But what if you looked at them straight on, with loving awareness, and without fear?

Personal Exploration #12: Sitting with your painful thoughts

Before contemplating the exercise below, please know that mental and emotional pain is just as real as physical pain. Just as you consult physicians for physical conditions, it is equally important and valuable to consult mental health professionals for emotional pain. The meditation below should in no way substitute for getting any medical treatment or mental health services you might need.

It's common for us to react to painful and recurring thoughts (such as shame, guilt, resentment, or blame), either struggling against them, finding proof for them, or rationalizing them. And sometimes we engage in denial, pretending that someone or something has not just *pushed our buttons*, explaining away whatever discomfort we will acknowledge. But all of these mental gymnastics only strengthen the power and authority of our stories, drawing our attention away from a tremendous opportunity for healing. Instead of adding to the feeding frenzy of the thinking mind, I invite you to instead explore the tremendous possibility for transparency, vulnerability, and clarity that these opportunities create.

First, simply recognize the painful thoughts that exist in your mind. Can you allow each thought to be, without struggling, or following, or rationalizing? Can you simply notice, and name your experience? If you have a lot of different thoughts, try choosing one by quietly asking, *What most needs to heal?* Or, as Pema Chödrön wrote, "What if you could open to that frustration, just for a moment, to discover not just where love is free flowing … but where it's not? That is how we all begin to uncover the soft spot within."

When you feel yourself out of balance and craving peace, see if you can simply recognize and allow that impulse to exist, without the mental scurrying to *make* peace happen. You can open space, welcoming your edge of resistance. This practice reveals the gift of receiving pain as an invitation. When your mind is screaming, *I want peace, but I feel frustrated…things aren't coming together as they should… I'm not regarded as I should be*, can you sit with that? Can you offer that frustration loving, unconditional spaciousness? That feeling of frustration (or remorse, or longing, or whatever painful emotion has arisen) is a blessedly bright neon sign, showing you where you are resisting whatever is present. In this pointing, it is a tremendous gift. For some of us, instead of real pain, our messages are felt more as numbness. So it may be that, for you, it is numbness more than pain that guides your healing.

As you continue on your path, becoming more aware of whatever is present for you, you may feel as if you are experiencing an increase in emotional pain. This increase in discomfort may be a sign that you are creating new patterns of mental activity, and you are becoming more aware of where you generate your strongest resistance.

When a person is in pain, sometimes the focus of that pain can be all-consuming. The mind imagines that nothing exists except that pain. In depression, it can be difficult to even imagine the possibility of ever feeling joyful again. And yet, if you are able to become a witness, by seeing the pain and willingly experiencing it fully without calling it "me," the pain itself becomes your friend and ally: it points to where you are grasping and rejecting what life offers. By becoming aware of where you resist the present, you have the opportunity to awaken, to let go of the egoic struggle pain has exposed, and to settle in the bliss of what is already present. A numbed life may seem more comfortable, but it doesn't offer the possibility of joy inherent in willingly employing your consciousness and utilizing pain as an ally for authentic living.

Mortality as inspiration

Death is the only wise advisor that we have.
Whenever you feel, as you always do, that everything is going
wrong and you're about to be annihilated, turn to your death
and ask if that is so. Your death will tell you that you're
wrong; that nothing really matters outside its touch.
Your death will tell you, 'I haven't touched you yet.'
—Carlos Castaneda—

I love it that resources variously classified as spiritual, fictional, historical, or medical often point to the same underlying truths. Some people feel more enriched by choosing a single path and following it to its end. While that perspective is valid and beautiful, I tend to be more eclectic, and I delight in the synchronicity of the many paths, the realization that many disciplines point to the same essential truths.

In college, I discovered the books of Carlos Castenada in a used bookstore in Berkeley. Castenada is a controversial anthropologist who wrote several books about his relationship with a Yaqui Indian from Mexico. In these books Castenada was portrayed as the reluctant student of the profound warrior, Don Juan. The books are, for the most part, eminently readable, both engaging and packed with beautiful insights. Because of the controversies surrounding the books, they can be found in the fictional, metaphysical, or anthropological sections of bookstores, a range that I find amusing due to my love for finding truth from many angles.

These books share many wonderful concepts, but one that stuck with me most deeply was the idea of *using your death as an advisor*. This idea isn't a gloomy fixation on self-pity regarding one's own mortality. Quite the opposite: it's a call to action. *Using death as an advisor* is rooted in the acknowledgement that most of us live our lives as if we expect to live forever. We *kill time* doing mindless activities, both physical and mental. From Don Juan's perspective, it is more enriching and fulfilling to live a conscious life, with every action performed as if it were the last. When you realize that you truly *could* die at any moment, your choices crystallize into a beautiful starkness: Who would choose as their last thought a small-minded complaint or petty grudge? Who would select as their last action mindless channel surfing or playing computer solitaire?

It's not that one must do celebrated gestures at every moment, such as closing huge business deals or donating large sums of money to worthy causes. In fact, the growing field of Near Death Experiences documents that most people who experience life reviews report that the grand gestures mean very little. Instead, the small kindnesses and slights, the subtle ways in which we impact each other's lives, have much more importance. When a stranger asks you for directions on the street, it matters that you give them a minute of your time to ensure they will get where they hope to be. It matters that you treat people with respect, and with gentleness.

The practice of using death as an advisor can permeate every area of your life. For example, when you walk your dog, knowing that this could be your last moment, you truly connect with the sky, the plants, the joy your canine friend experiences in discovering scent trails. When you are having a conversation with a loved one, you truly hear what they are saying, conversing heart-to-heart. You let go of knee jerk reactions, knowing that you would not choose a spiteful retort for your final gesture. If you notice any smallness arising in your mind (pettiness, anger, jealousy, or blame, for example), you contemplate the thought from the perspective of your own death: in the face of that immensity, does that thought still hold your attention? Can you instead merely recognize and acknowledge it, and allow its grip on your mind to dissolve?

People with different perspectives point to this same awareness in various ways: living with mindfulness, presence, or awareness. And there are many profound and beautiful ways to approach this central knowing. People who find those other concepts elusive can truly deepen into presence by practicing using death as an advisor, since it has a tangibility to it that can feel far more real.

Often, we don't really contemplate our own deaths until forced to confront a life-threatening situation such as a terminal illness or some other physical danger. Of course, life itself is a terminal condition. From a shallow view, contemplating one's own death can seem like a morbid fixation. On the other hand, when contemplated with the appropriate reverence and depth, death can be an incredible motivator, inspiring us to break through walls of fear and doubt, guiding us towards our deepest, truest Self.

Personal Exploration #13:   Using death as an advisor

How would you live your life differently if you knew that you only had a year to live? What would you change if you only had a month? Perhaps, from the perspective of your own mortality, you can see trifling matters in your life. Can you let them go? Perhaps you feel your work no longer fits you, and yet you continue going through the motions. Would you explore investing your time and energy in a career with deeper resonance for you? Perhaps you feel inspired to create a *bucket list* of skills or experiences that you would like to explore before your death. Is there a saxophone gathering dust in your closet? Why not take lessons? Have you always wanted to take your children or spouse to your beloved hometown lake? Why not plan a family trip? Do you feel the impulse to learn to meditate? There is truly no time like the present. Do you love spending time with animals? Why not foster rescues if it's not the right time for you to adopt a pet?

If you knew this were your last day, how would you invest your time and energy? If you knew that you would die in the next few minutes, what would you choose as your last gesture? What state of mind would you like to have when you pass? Why not choose those investments, those gestures, those states of mind right now?

What last impression or gift would you leave for others? Knowing that you will die, what changes would you make to embrace your life more fully?

Welcoming fear

> *You can fail at what you don't want,*
> *so why not take a chance at doing what you love?*
> —*Jim Carrey*—

Poet Rainer Maria Rilke wrote that fear is the dragon that guards your greatest treasures. Fear can guide us towards what we most need to explore, and to where we may most beneficially grow. Fear also warns us that we need to prepare, that we need to train hard and sweat the details. I'm not a huge fan of fearlessness. But, courage in the face of fear is beautiful. By working *through* our fears, we discover our hidden gifts. You've surely had the experience of doing something that you knew was beneficial but that you also felt afraid to do. Doing it successfully despite your fear most likely resulted in exhilaration and personal growth. It may well also have revealed new talents and interests you never suspected, or perhaps suspected but did not believe. Fear is not a problem. Rather, it can be a tremendous helper when met with courage, will power, and dedication to truth. Obviously, nothing can protect us from bodily mortality. Still, we are here now—and that is enough. We *could* allow fear to confine us into smaller and smaller boxes. On the other hand, breaking through fear shatters the walls that confine us, revealing our hidden beauty.

Leveraging mirrors for deeper understanding

I was surprised and excited to find this beautiful explanation of perception in a biopsychology textbook:

Imagine that you are a piece of iron. I admit that's not easy to do. A piece of iron doesn't have a brain, and even if it did it wouldn't have much experience. But try to imagine it anyway.

So, there you are, sitting around doing nothing, as usual, when along comes a drop of water. What will be your perception, your experience of the water?

You will have the experience of rust. From your point of view, water is above all else rustish. Now return to your perspective as a human. You know that rustishness is not really a property of water itself but of the way water interacts with iron.

The same is true of human perception. In vision, for example, when you look at the leaves of a tree, you perceive them as green. But green is no more a property of the leaves themselves than rustish is a property of water. The greenness is what happens when the light bouncing off the leaves interacts with the neurons in the back of your eye, and eventually with the neurons in your brain. That is, the greenness is really in us—just as the rust is really in the piece of iron.

Republished with permission of South-Western College Publishing, A Division Of Cengage Learning, from Biological Psychology, James W. Kalat, Sixth Edition, 1998; permission conveyed through Copyright Clearance Center, Inc.

As this section came out of a biopsychology textbook, it was meant quite literally. Still, it is equally true of non-physical phenomena. So often, our perceptions of people and events reflect more about ourselves than the apparent object of our reflections. In self-discovery, we often talk about this phenomenon as encountering others as mirrors of ourselves. When we meet people who inspire us, who have traits that we admire, it is useful to notice how those traits can be seen in ourselves. Conversely, when we meet people who demonstrate qualities that we find distasteful, it is just as (perhaps even more) useful to look within, and to notice where we exhibit those same traits. When we meet people who push our buttons, it is useful to lovingly investigate our internal source of irritation. The idea behind mirrors is that we often see in others shortcomings that we'd prefer not to notice in ourselves.

When you pay attention, you can see that your own unconscious behavior is reflected back to you by your family and your community. That is, when you are acting unconsciously, the people around you tend to respond in ways that reflect your own state of mind. Happily, this reflection is a tremendously useful tool: you can use it to remind yourself to behave more consciously.

For example, consider anger. Cranky people tend to annoy other people, and so meet with more hostility in their daily interactions. In turn, that hostility feeds the cranky person's anger. The good news is that we have the power to change even deep-seated mental patterns. We do so by first beginning to watch the mind, paying attention to the mind's shifting winds. We then choose equanimity when the familiar seeds of anger sprout. In this way, we can actually re-wire our reactions, choosing peace and wellness. With careful attention, anger can become a progressively less common state of mind.

Or consider fear. A person who makes a habit of avoiding intimidating situations typically becomes more fearful and timid. The people with whom they interact register that fear and reflect it back. Sometimes they resonate with a fearful person by becoming nervous, unsure, or uncomfortable themselves. On the other hand, they might reflexively react with aggression. The fearful person has generated a pattern of shrinking from adventures and opportunities, and that pattern is reinforced each time they shrink back. Again, there is good news. Such people have the power to change by consciously switching patterns, as by trying new things even (or especially) when they are intimidating. This is one of the basic understandings underlying the field of cognitive behavioral psychotherapy. Over time, new mental states of trust and adventure can be consciously developed.

Mirrors reflect our positive unconscious perspectives as well. For example, consider kindness and peacefulness. Peaceful, present people tend to encourage such states of mind in others. The small kindnesses they extend throughout the day are often reflected back with gentleness and loving attention. Peaceful people also meet challenges with the silent knowledge that they have whatever they need to respond with ease and grace.

The practice of utilizing mirrors usually involves some temporary psychological pain, because it encourages us to intentionally expose and study our shadows (including our assumptions, aversions, attachments, and aspects of ourselves that we would rather not acknowledge). This practice allows us to discover an awesomely beautiful freedom. By utilizing mirrors to see our shadows, we learn to recognize hidden aspects of ourselves, and this recognition provides the opportunity to invite our shadows into the light. By lighting our shadows, by surrounding them with loving awareness, we dissolve the tension and pain involved in hiding from aspects of ourselves.

My root meditation teacher often said, "Recognition is dissolution." It takes courage to be willing to look within to see your habitual patterns. Because of our mental tendencies, it can seem much easier to ignore such shortcomings and to shrink your life in a way that doesn't expose the raw edges. However, even though it is largely unconscious, there is actually quite a lot of work in such patterns of avoidance—work that takes energy that can be put to much better use. In addition to reclaiming our energy, discovering and releasing the habitual patterns gives profound insights and experiences of freedom, love, and joy.

The concept of mirrors also makes it much easier to have compassion for others. Have you ever had someone assume the worst, accusing you of harmful intentions or actions? When I've been in those positions, I first look through the mirror at myself, searching for thought patterns that I have hidden from view. If I have an emotional reaction to the charge, I know that there is likely something deeper to investigate. If not, I typically find that I'm simply serving as a mirror for that person. For example, I might be reflecting back their own fears or past experiences that they haven't finished working through. It can be easy to be offended by this sort of misunderstanding. And yet, when viewed through the lens of mirrors, the obvious reaction is one of compassion. Often, simple misunderstandings can be cleared up with a heart-based conversation. But, at times, I've found that the person is simply dealing with their own demons, which can be a painful and confusing process, especially when they aren't ready to see the image in the mirror.

I've learned how critically important it is for each person to see and work with their own mirrors in their own time. There are places where we can help each other out, but when it comes to self-discovery, the most important help we can offer is to work on ourselves. Our own internal work creates loving space that benefits others as they do their processing. In this loving space, we are able to be present for others by seeing them for who they are, and not mistaking them for their unconscious reactions—or for our own unconscious projections, for that matter. By developing the perspective of loving awareness, we can perceive a loved one's confusion, while simultaneously witnessing and providing loving space for the light within.

Personal Exploration #14: Utilizing mirrors for growth

Your mirrors can be incredibly useful to you. They show you where you grasp and where you resist. And by recognizing these places and investigating them without fighting or clinging, you come to recognize other people's mirrors for what they are, and not as threats. There are several ways to use mirrors to discover unconscious aspects of yourself, if you choose to look courageously within.

Reflecting on what *everyone* does

When you notice yourself having thoughts or making statements like, *Everyone is acting so angrily towards me!* or *Everyone is projecting their issues onto me!* or any similar complaints with the implicit message that *they* are treating me unfairly, you've just stumbled across an incredibly valuable piece of information. In using mirrors, you can simply take that complaint, flip the participants, and rephrase it as a question. For example, *How and in what way am I throwing anger at others?* or *Which issue am I projecting onto others and how am I doing it?* With mindfulness, it becomes obvious that *they* are not your problem; *they* are in fact the very mirrors you need to discover the egoic mechanisms you use to cause pain for yourself and for others. In that discovery, and in the subsequent dissolving of those mechanisms, you will find peace, space, and freedom.

Reflecting on personal relationships using mirrors

Statements about what *everyone* is doing are especially telling, since it is far more likely that the issue is with you than with *everyone* you encounter. However, mirrors can be incredibly useful in one-on-one relationships as well. When someone treats you in a way you don't like, the natural human reaction is to find fault in their behavior. It is, however, much more interesting and revealing to investigate the interaction from the perspective of mirrors. Such questions could include:

- *In what ways does my behavior reflect the behavior I am resenting in this person?*
- *What aspects of my attitudes or my behavior generate this sort of reaction?*
- *Why do I think I need this person to be a particular way?*
- *What is it that I imagine I lack?*

In the same way, what you see as lacking in others suggests things that you imagine are lacking in yourself. For example, let's say that you love helping others, and you put that urge into action. So far, so good. However, if you notice yourself getting resentful, perhaps wishing that your efforts were more valued, you can choose to see the mirror in the situation—that the problem at that moment might not be the other person's ingratitude but that you feel a need to be appreciated.

And again, in recognizing that tendency in yourself, you can choose to release it, realizing that whether you are acknowledged or ignored is an egoic concern, an assumption of an imagined deficiency that has no bearing on your deeper consciousness. Of course, it is possible that your reflections will result in the realization that you need to adjust or end a relationship. But before focusing on what may need to change outwardly, I invite you to explore the possibility of what you may profit from changing or releasing inwardly.

Using mirrors to illuminate your patterns

Mirrors may also reflect issues from your past. How often do you notice yourself saying that someone is *just like* someone you resent from your past? It is doubtful that you've met anyone who is *just like* anyone, past or present. In such cases, it is far more likely that people serve as mirrors, triggering your own unresolved issues. Such episodes are an invitation to truth. Although the natural human tendency is to leave the fault in *their* hands, it is much more useful to discover and release whatever they trigger instead. There's a Tibetan proverb that goes, *It's much easier to wear shoes than to pave the world with leather.* By trying to avoid everyone who pushes our buttons in some way, we lop off piece after piece of our world. But if we explore our edges by acknowledging our recurring patterns while refusing to act on them, we empower ourselves to recognize, allow, and release dysfunctional misperceptions and distorted reactions.

Investigating whatever is revealed

Once you have a juicy topic for inquiry, it's time to enlist our practices for recognition and allowing (*Personal Exploration #8: Recognition and allowing*). The purpose of working with mirrors for self-inquiry is emphatically not to uncover another club to beat ourselves up with, or another hook to hang our self-doubt on. Instead, we are simply using mirrors to support our investigation into the ways we are reacting unconsciously. We enlist our ground of loving awareness, acceptance, and compassion to see where we need an adjustment. Frequently, the act of recognition and allowing is sufficient: the power of our trigger is dissolved. Sometimes we need deeper investigation.

> Of course, this practice is not a tacit agreement that you should stay in an unhealthy or unsafe relationship. It's simply a first step to gain clarity into your own unconscious patterns, so that whatever action you take is rooted in discernment rather than unconscious reflexes.

Putting aside the shovel

When new political scandals make the rounds on news outlets, I often hear the adage, *If you find you're in a hole, first, stop digging.* I love this expression; it's tidy, quick, and packed with funny images. However, colorful expressions aside, it is all too easy to overlook our position when we in fact are in a hole, and it can be difficult to see how we are digging ourselves deeper. For example, a vascular surgeon once mentioned to me that patients frequently complained to him about their pain. He'd tell them that they needed to begin an exercise program, and they often reacted incredulously, saying, "But I'm in *pain.*" Of course, some pains *do* require rest, some pains *are* lessened by massage, and some pains *are* masked by pharmaceuticals. But the stagnation that sets into a body that isn't well-exercised causes a kind of pain that is truly best addressed with gentle exercise (with the doctor's approval, of course).

Mental pain also has various potential remedies. You can try to avoid the things that challenge you, you can try to mask the pain (for example, with shopping or alcohol), or you can make adjustments to address the underlying causes. While some issues are easily identified and corrected, it's much harder to address conditions that are aptly characterized as *malaise*, conditions in which everything seems to be okay, and yet you still aren't happy.

In a way, living in the West is a set up for this sort of malaise. Most of us have access to everything we really need in terms of our physical well-being. And yet, of course, the spirit wants more than an adequate physical existence. We live in the land of marketing, and are told that so many different things will finally make us genuinely happy: toothpaste, stylish cars, beer, kids, picket fences, career advancement, the "right" religion, the "right" partner, or the perfect couch. And there is no shortage of advice. Self-help books fly off the shelves. Mega-churches have literally thousands of people in attendance each Sunday. Talk shows, advice columnists, and others hop onto the bandwagon.

The problem is that one size never fits all. Being in tune with your own mental patterns and watching them dispassionately can make it a lot easier to sort through the thousands of suggestions in order to explore the essence of whatever it is that you most need to shift. Acknowledging your own unhelpful patterns gives you a starting point for effecting change. Acknowledging mistakes is not always easy, but in the end, if followed by appropriate adjustments, it is much more satisfying than ignoring them.

Sometimes, there's just no substitute for insights from a dear friend or a trusted confidante (such as a teacher, life coach, Zen guide, parent, or psychologist). Sometimes, even though you notice that you sure seem to be covered with a lot of dirt, it can be incredibly difficult to notice that *you* are holding the shovel (and you may suspect someone else is shoveling dirt on you). You may even realize you are in fact the digger, but have no idea how you are wielding the shovel.

So having someone who can lovingly help you to recognize unconscious habitual patterns can be quite a blessing. Similarly, even if you can see the mechanisms and know the changes that you need to make, self-doubts rise up, particularly when the changes will affect others. In such instances it's useful to have someone you trust to confirm your observations and path or, perhaps, to help you to discover a solution you haven't yet considered. Change is often difficult, even when it is a change for the better. For all of these reasons, it is helpful to have friends who encourage you along the path of personal growth.

Still, even though it's incredibly beneficial to have trusted guides and fellow travelers on the road to self-discovery, you are still the only one who can do your work. Whether you discover your mechanism of digging yourself or a loved one helps you see it, you are still the one who needs to quit digging and put down the shovel. By enlisting your courage and discipline, and by employing discernment and loving awareness, you have what you need to set down your shovel and walk your authentic path.

Compassion

If you want others to be happy, practice compassion.
If you want to be happy, practice compassion.
—Dalai Lama—

The root of compassion

My boyfriend has a PhD in psychology. I love our conversations, which commingle Western psychology and medicine and Eastern philosophy—flowing, integrating, and differentiating, as we explore ways of understanding life. Once, as we listened together to an interview with Roshi Joan Halifax, he said something that beautifully revealed a truth that was so much a part of my conception of Being that I hadn't thought to name it. "Buddhism and humanistic psychology have so much in common, so many similar ideas of how minds work," he mused. "The difference, I think, is that Buddhists believe that everyone is, fundamentally [at our core, and most truly], Love." My mind stopped for a moment; I sat across from him, silently reveling in his discovery. After savoring the moment, I smiled, nodded, and felt love flood my being.

Perhaps because of its limited acknowledgement of human interconnectedness, Western psychology doesn't explore love in the same way as Eastern philosophy. In the Eastern mind, love is ever present, just below the surface, eager to burst through. One of my boyfriend's favorite insights from his school counseling days is that *unconditional positive regard* can heal more readily and more profoundly than any knowledge, strategy, or technique that can be taught. But what is, one wonders, the source of that *unconditional positive regard*, that *love*? Love is always present and always accessible; it inhabits the gaps between our thoughts, our reactions, our judgments, and our ideas of separation. Meditation and mindfulness are incredible tools for breaking free from mental activity that sometimes feels uncontrollable; they expand the gaps and increase our opportunity to explore the innate gift of the presence of love.

In the course of our journey together, we've explored many beautiful forms of meditative practice. A practice that we have not yet discussed, one that opens welcome spaciousness for me, is a meditative yoga flow. In this practice, I reflect on the current experience of each successive moment to the best of my ability. I begin and periodically return to a sincere *check-in*: Is my mind anywhere beyond my mat, making grocery lists, replaying events? Do I feel unnecessary bodily tension, perhaps indicating stress at a subconscious level? If I detect irrelevant mental activity during this check, I invite release and re-focus my mind on the moment. Practicing in this way, I repeatedly return to the inquiry, *What will best serve my body and mind in this moment?* Entering poses gently and mindfully, I get into a flow, sometimes adding more challenge, sometimes extending and deepening my breath, sometimes resting into stillness as the class flows around me. Each moment I explore whatever movement or non-movement feels most authentic, grateful for the grace in the timeless transitions between postures.

I've found that this practice in awareness sharpens my intuition and boosts my compassionate responsiveness to others. Slowing down mental activity enough to feel the contours of the moment, as well as appreciating moment-to-moment transitions, are beneficial off the mat or on it. Such practice re-trains the mind for greater presence, opening the possibility of purer resonance to and compassion for myself and others. I've found that the practice of yoga flow allows me to enter more completely into everything from making simple choices like where to have dinner with a friend, more complex decisions like career moves, or deeply consequential decisions, like commitments in my relationships with significant others. Practicing sincere, gentle, responsive compassion for myself provides a wonderful opportunity to learn to appreciate the gift of having space to explore and to grow.

A Compassionately light touch

Interacting with others, we can easily feel compelled to *fix* whatever we imagine needs fixing. And yet, providing the loving space to let others process their own issues is essential for their deepening understanding. Providing loving support for others as they struggle to find their highest (or truest) path is far more beneficial to friends and loved ones than attempting to solve their problems for them.

Helping a baby bird as it breaks through its shell greatly diminishes its chances for survival. When wildlife rehabilitators help animals recover, they make maintaining and increasing self-reliance a primary goal. When wise parents see their children struggle with homework, instead of doing the work themselves, they provide the loving support that tips the scales in favor of growth. I love the phrase, *setting others up for success*, as it is so descriptive of this process. Our helpfulness is most fruitful when we couple compassion and awareness with patience and the faith that our loved one is capable of finding his own sacred path. For me, true compassion has a light touch. It is the profoundly joyful experience of feeling another as a part of myself, and instinctively responding with unconditional love.

Personal Exploration #15:   Loving-kindness meditation

I find the *loving-kindness* meditation to be a beautiful practice, especially when I'm too much in my head and need to reconnect with my heart. To begin this practice, first find your meditative seat (see *Personal Exploration #4: Finding your meditative seat* for steps). Next, take a few slow, deep breaths, with your mind attending as fully as possible to your breath. Now, visualize expanding and softening through your heart. If that's too abstract, visualize breathing into or through your heart. If you aren't quite sure where to feel your heart, simply bring your finger to your center, pointing to "me." Some of us point a little higher or lower than others. Wherever your finger naturally lands is your perfect location.

To begin the loving-kindness (or, *Metta*) meditation, first meditate on loving-kindness for yourself. We start with ourselves because it is difficult to feel lovingly towards others when our self-love is limited.

While continuing to visualize breathing through your heart, mentally repeat, *May I be filled with loving-kindness. May I be safe from inner and outer dangers. May I be well in body and mind. May I be peaceful and at ease.* I've found many versions of these sentiments, so feel free to adapt them, using loving-kindness as your guide. Feel the intention these words express. Consciously recognize feelings of affinity, joy, and love as they arise. Don't feel as if you need to *do* anything to *bring about* love, or safety, or peace. Instead, simply see yourself as a conduit, a channel through which blessings flow, and a witness to their presence.

When you feel ready, the next step is to meditate on someone who has cared deeply for you. You may bring to mind a dear friend, a child, a parent, a pet, or a spiritual teacher. For this second step, you'll want to choose someone towards whom you feel unequivocally loving. Choose whoever feels most natural for you. With this person in mind, mentally repeat similar statements, directed at your loved one. *May you be filled with loving-kindness. May you be safe from inner and outer dangers. May you be well in body and mind. May you be peaceful and at ease.* Practice non-attachment: Rather than feeling attached to a specific effect or outcome, simply invite and witness blessings as they flow from the field of loving awareness. Again, be attentive to feelings of loving-kindness as they arise. This sense of connection to warm feelings is beneficial because it helps these feelings to deepen in your mind and heart.

When you are ready, bring to mind others in an expanding circle, calling to mind those for whom you have less innately warm regards. For example, you may reach progressively from friends and family, to neighbors, acquaintances, strangers, people with whom you've had difficulties, and eventually to all sentient beings. But start with those for whom you naturally feel the most affection, and then gradually expand your focus as your feeling of loving-kindness grows. You may use the same phrasing, or you may follow your intuition to discover a blessing that better represents how you feel. Continue to begin your well wishes with the phrase "may you..." to reinforce the understanding that you are a *conduit* for these blessings, and not the *doer*. You are simply, and beautifully, witnessing loving-kindness as it naturally unfolds.

You may notice as you meditate that feelings of grief, anger, or sadness arise. These feelings can be the natural responses of an opening heart. You may feel drawn to mindfully witness them, shining your light of recognition on them. Or you may choose to direct your loving-kindness to these feelings themselves, or to return to the first step, wishing loving-kindness for yourself. As much as possible, don't struggle against these feelings, or banish them, or get lost in them. Simply open your loving, conscious witnessing to them. As always, follow your intuition, powered by love and wisdom. When your meditation feels complete, you might like to seal your practice with a bow of gratitude for whatever has arisen.

Compassion fatigue

Recall once more our monk from the traditional tale who repeatedly scooped a scorpion towards safety and was repeatedly stung in the process. When we think that helping others, or that being present with others who are in pain, is necessarily painful for ourselves, we create walls of separation. The unconscious stories we tell ourselves are often something like, "*they* are painful (or, *toxic),* *I* am spiritual (or *wise*), and *I'm* willing to help *them.*" There are several problems with this version of compassion, from my perspective. It typically causes pain for ourselves and others, since it's based on, and strengthens, stories of fear and resistance (ours and theirs) rather than the direct experience of loving awareness. It is rooted in being judgmental rather than discerning, and so lacks wisdom. Moreover, one lesson we often learn from this version of compassion is that being present for someone is painful, or, at a minimum, exhausting. *Compassion fatigue*, the gradual lessening of compassion over time, often combined with diffuse feelings of resentment and stress, sets in.

So, how do you develop compassion without getting lost in stories and judgment? How do you maintain an open heart, rather than collapsing into compassion fatigue? I've found that it is incredibly useful for each of us to examine our *own* stories of lack, or limitation—or superiority, for that matter. These stories represent beliefs about what we imagine *is* or *should be.* They cause us pain when they suggest we must reject or fight against whatever is present. We can find freedom and ease if we question and discard those stories that send us chasing our tails with guilt, worry, shame, or other heavy emotions. And yet, when it comes to having *compassion for others*, our most skillful role is very different.

To support others by dissecting *their* belief systems can be a resentment-generating and counterproductive approach. But providing nonjudgmental, loving presence (or, *unconditional positive regard*) is a less intrusive, and more effective, response to the stories of fear, lack, or need that distress our friends and loved ones. Each of us has blind spots, as well as perspectives from which we see clearly. Compassion is the affirmation of those perspectives from which our friends can see lucidly, as well as the provision of loving understanding and empathy for the perceptions that feel confused and painful. When we try to fix someone, or we fall apart with them, or we recoil from them as if they were toxic, we actually energize painful beliefs instead of creating space and shining light to support healing.

Light-based compassion is about empathizing with people for the pain that their beliefs cause them, without necessarily believing their stories. It is about giving people sacred space to explore their own understandings. But in doing so we are challenged to shift our perspective, letting go of our *own* ideas of how things *should* be, while simultaneously keeping our hearts open.

Light-based compassion requires a light touch. Other people's ideas of how things are or should be are real to them; these ideas generate very real pain for the people that hold them. To really help them, our role is to be with them as they explore their stories, offering compassionate insights as the opportunity arises. The key, though, is to feel empathy *without* either lending some form of credence to the stories or slipping into painful states of mind, such as depression, fury, or guilt. To be truly helpful, we create space for each other to see that what we believe is always only a small measure of the truth—a truth that is, in human interactions, always subjective. And, that space is held with unconditional love.

To the casual observer, light-based compassion and run-of-the-mill compassion look similar. Outwardly, both may involve being present, practicing empathy, offering food or money to others who would benefit from it, and truly hearing their stories. Someone paying a little more attention might notice that light-based compassion looks a little less agreeable, because it doesn't indulge any of the painful stories of guilt, blame, resentment or futility. But the main difference is internal: in light-based compassion, you constantly maintain the awareness of the spiritual underpinning of reality. With light-based compassion, we embody Pierre Teilhard de Chardin's insight, "We are not human beings having a spiritual experience. We are spiritual beings having a human experience."

You don't have to believe other peoples' stories (all those painful ideas about why they can't be happy) any more than you do your own. Instead, you can simply feel that, "Yes, it would be painful to believe that that is who you are, or how you must be limited." And, in that space, you rest in unconditionally loving awareness.

This shift in attitude creates space for change, since you deeply embrace your awareness that others are more than the sum total of their beliefs. A tremendous upwelling of empathy accompanies this shift because you understand how challenging it is to feel like such a fragile, limited being. You also come to appreciate that we are all equal, that you are in no way better than someone whose stories you can see through. This realistic humility is reinforced as, over time, you realize that it is always easier to see through other people's stories than your own, and that it's pretty likely someone else sees through yours. Finally, this empathy for others eventually works its way around to you, and you begin to feel deeper compassion for yourself.

Becoming love

My root meditation teacher once gave an inspiring lecture on the topic of love. He said that people imagine that they want to be loved, and therefore search arduously for their *ideal match*. They may find someone, or they may not. Regardless of the success of that search, they work hard to be loved, perhaps spending their whole lives trying to become somehow more lovable—more financially successful, more physically attractive, more attentive, or any other sort of improvement they believe their mate (real or imagined) would find attractive.

Of course, it is beautiful to grow and to be successful. My teacher's point was simply that, when we orient our lives towards what we think we need from others, we base our happiness and peace on external factors, such as how others react to us. We give away our freedom by orienting ourselves towards what others want from us, and by so doing we inadvertently drive love away.

The moment we notice the thought, "I'd be happy if only he/she would…" is the moment we can truly see where we've misplaced our trust, anchoring it to another's reactions rather than on our own open heart. Our peace and happiness is not dependent on the understandings or impressions of someone else. How could it be? Our peace is as profound as our presence—and potentially as limitless as eternity.

In truth, we want to be Love itself. And in that, there is no waiting, no doing, and no depending on another's doing. What is required is simply the abandonment of grasping and striving. This renunciation, by its very nature, allows the heart to open naturally to Love, Light, God, Eternity—to whatever you call that which speaks most deeply to you. And there is tremendous freedom in choosing to let go of expectations and desires, to fully meet the Present with a smile and an open heart, becoming Love itself.

Personal Exploration #16:   Blossoming heart meditation

To begin this practice, first find your meditative seat (see *Personal Exploration #4: Finding your meditative seat* for steps). Now, intuitively feel your heart. If you aren't quite sure where to feel your heart, simply bring your finger to your center, pointing to "me." In your heart space, visualize a small, bright pink flower bud forming. As you inhale, visualize light passing through the back of your heart into the bud, gently opening it more and more. As you exhale, rest in the loving awareness of the opening blossom. As you continue to breathe in this manner, visualize your flower blossoming, unfolding into an exquisite flower. Perhaps you visualize a bright pink blossom with numerous petals, like a rose or a peony; or maybe you see something simpler, like a lily or lotus flower. As you meditate, feel the Light of the universe (or God, or Goddess, or Love) filling your heart. When your mediation feels complete, allow the flower to dissolve. Perhaps you'd like to seal your practice with a bow of gratitude for whatever has arisen.

Forgiveness

> *In the end these things matter most: How well did you love?*
> *How fully did you live? How deeply did you let go?*
> —*Gautama Buddha*—

When we allow unforgiving attitudes to solidify, they tend to empower our ego, either reinforcing feelings of superiority and self-righteousness, or feelings of personal vulnerability and inadequacy. Being swept away by the ego in either direction blocks the development of true humility as well as our awareness of our intimate connection with the Ultimate—with Light, Love, Eternity, God, Goddess, or whatever speaks most closely to our heart.

Investigating forgiveness

> *Thought is the sculptor who can create*
> *the person you want to be.*
> —*Henry David Thoreau*—

There are many useful cognitive techniques for working through non-forgiveness and towards letting go. Compassion and discernment are essential components for any of these specific methods or practices. One technique that I have found to be tremendously useful is to hold space for myself and others by accepting each of us as being a "work in progress." I let go of my ideas of how things *should* be, and I try to see how someone—me or someone else—is actually doing the best he can given the skills and awareness he has at the time.

Of course, forgiveness doesn't mean staying in an unsafe situation or repeating the same mistakes. It is essential that we act with discernment, honestly assessing situations and making appropriate adjustments. In particular, when forgiving ourselves for past mistakes, an essential next step is to reassess, adjust as needed, and to live as mindfully as possible with a new pattern of being. When we live mindfully, putting forth "right effort" the first time around, sweating the details (and knowing when we need a break), we'll feel a much greater sense of ease and gentleness while being out in the world. And there will be fewer things for which we need to forgive ourselves.

As I reflect on forgiveness, I realize that, for me, it occurs at a few levels. I can consciously forgive someone for some perceived offense, or myself for some shortcoming or mistake, while still holding onto non-forgiveness unconsciously. I can feel this unconscious non-forgiveness as tension in my body. When I think about the person or situation, I might feel tightness in a specific area, such as my heart, forehead, or gut. Only when I truly feel gentleness in my body, with no increase in tension when a person, situation, or event comes to mind, do I know that I've stepped more completely into true forgiveness.

Seated meditation can be a profoundly useful practice for breaking through non-forgiveness. In this practice, I have found that it is counterproductive to "think through" whatever is on my mind while in meditation. There is certainly a place for that type of mental activity; it can be useful to think through one's past, whether alone, with a psychologist, or with a dear friend. However, in meditation, I've found that that sort of cognitive processing gets in the way. Instead, I've found that it is much more useful to let go of the story entirely. Since non-forgiveness has a specific sort of tension in my body, I have found seated meditation with visualization and body awareness to be far more helpful in unwinding those sorts of *knots*.

Personal Exploration #17:   Somatic forgiveness visualization

To begin this practice, first find your meditative seat (see *Personal Exploration #4: Finding your meditative seat* for steps). Then, visualize grounding deeply into the earth, extending roots that reach through the crust and into the molten core. While maintaining that connection, feel within your body for points of tension and visualize flushing the knots out, watching the tension travel down your roots and dissolve in magma, purifying and transforming into light. As the knots soften and release, visualize light coming through the crown of your head, filling the now cleared space with light (I'll often visualize golden or pink light, but please use whatever color feels most appropriate for you). Continue releasing tension and inviting Light to fill its void until you sense the tension has been purified and cleared. When your meditation feels complete, re-seal by dissolving your roots and sealing the crown of your head. You may choose to conclude this practice with an offering of gratitude.

Letting go and letting Light shine

When I can truly feel gratitude for a person or situation, or for myself, in regard to the ways that I once held resentment or fear, I know that forgiveness has occurred. There are many techniques to invite forgiveness to take root and unfold, and many are quite helpful. But the essential starting point for true forgiveness is to love the direct experience of Light—or, Eternity, God, Goddess, "peace beyond all understanding," or whatever concept speaks most closely to your heart. Forgiveness comes when we love the Light more than we feel driven to cling to our grievances or feelings of limitation. Although this is obvious when we think about it, we nevertheless benefit from reflection to regain our perspective, and training to maintain it. Techniques can be helpful in regaining that state of ease, love, and gratitude that, I feel, is our natural way of being.

FURTHER EXPLORATIONS IN AUTHENTICITY

Charting Your Spirit's Path

When you do things from your soul,
you feel a river moving in you, a joy.
—Rumi—

Empowering yourself and others

Service to others is the rent you pay
for your room here on earth.
—Muhammad Ali—

Perhaps you have some negative ideas about power. Throughout life, you've probably seen instances when power was misused. So, I feel it's important to reflect on the difference between "power to" versus "power over." "Power over" is the power that says I will hurt you, or control you, or make your life miserable if you don't think or feel or act as I think you should think or feel or act. "Power to" is its opposite. "Power to" opens space for ourselves and others to grow, and to shine. "Power to" provides love-filled light to our shadows, softening the grip of painful thoughts like blame, guilt, resentment, shame, or regret.

When we embrace our authentic path and act from truth, compassion, and wisdom in each moment, the door to empowerment opens for us and for those with whom we interact. Tapping into our truth leads to a cascade of positive change in our life, as well as in the lives of those we touch. So often, it's our *ideas*—our notions of who we are, who others should be, and life's inadequacies—that prevent power from flowing. Empowerment requires softening our grip on concepts of how things *should* be, opening space for truth and love to shine through.

We all have ideas about who we are. We might define ourselves as introverts or party girls; intellectuals or athletes; people who are sweet or short-tempered, strong-willed or frail. None of these categories is inherently and necessarily self-limiting. For instance, a short-tempered person can harness his emotional volatility and aggressiveness into becoming an effective and efficient leader in a fast-paced industry; the frail person can study debilities and their treatment, eventually blossoming into a powerful healer; and the social butterfly can learn to put her networking skills to work by creating exceptional opportunities for the community.

However, when we allow our self-identities to lock us into a rigid persona, we overlook our authentic paths and thereby forfeit opportunities for empowerment for ourselves and others. The party girl overlooks opportunities for meaningful connections; the introvert doesn't speak up when his or her voice is needed; the accomplished athlete misses opportunities to help clumsy children in learning to love physical play for itself; and the sweet person gets swindled by trusting a scoundrel.

When we cling to our ideas rigidly, we also typically impose our expectations on loved ones, friends, and even strangers, and we get frustrated when they don't meet our ideas of who they should be, what they should want, or how they should structure their lives. Too often we struggle to make others fit into the boxes we've created for them, either with pointless internal monologues or with actual arguments that never end well and always leave us feeling drained.

We also might have ideas about what life should look like. Perhaps we're attached to having a happy marriage with kids, a big house, a comfortable, financially rewarding job, a strong social network, and good health. The flip side of those ideas are the things we fear, such as losing our health, struggling to make ends meet, and dying alone. Giving in to these twin impulses by clinging to our desires and running away from our fears drains our personal power. Too often, we run in both directions at once and become exhausted and unbalanced, feeling stretched too thin without seeing the root cause.

When you let your *ideas* drive your life, especially fear-based ideas like fear of financial stress, isolation, or physical pain, it is easy to stray from your authentic path. But by training yourself to quiet your mind's restless activity and to rest in spacious compassion instead of mindlessly reacting to your fears, you will find it is much easier to see your path and to walk it with gratitude and grace.

Quieting your thinking mind and listening to your heart

To be yourself in a world that is constantly trying to make
you something else is the greatest accomplishment.
—Ralph Waldo Emerson—

Many of us chart our lives according to the expectations and examples of friends, families, or communities. We might go to college (or skip it) simply because everyone else we know is heading in that direction. We might feel antsy about taking the *next step*, into marriage, or having kids, or starting a business, after our friends have moved away from us down their particular path, perhaps urging us to do the same. At other times our lives are driven by the fear that we'd better take what's available or risk ending up with nothing.

So, when you feel pushed or pulled in a particular direction, how can you tell if you're being driven by outside pressure, by fear, or by an authentic calling? When you want to grow in ways your friends are growing, your desire for change could be motivated by feelings of competition, or by the fear of being left behind, or by a simple lack of creativity. On the other hand, you might be feeling the motivation that wells up when you witness a kind of growth in someone else that truly resonates with your spirit. How do you access the intuitive wisdom to be able to discriminate between fear-based reactivity and authentic aspiration?

There are different ways to receive the messages of intuition. Some of us receive messages visually. For example, when I received the intuition that I needed to move from New York, I set the intention that I would move once I felt clear about the destination. I suddenly saw "Boulder, Colorado" in books, advertisements, magazines, and movies. The town didn't exist for me one moment, and in the next, there were reminders everywhere I looked. When I notice that something suddenly appears strongly in my visual awareness, especially after setting an intention, I take notice of the message. I researched the town after its insistent arrival in my mind's eye. What I found suggested that Boulder would provide welcome opportunities for growth.

Other people tend to receive answers as bodily sensations, feeling contraction and expansion, or discomfort and relief, as they contemplate possibilities. As you consciously orient your life towards authenticity, the exercises below will support you in shaping a life that feels genuine for you. These exercises are most successfully performed after working with the preceding personal explorations, since the investigations below are empowered by your blossoming mindfulness, wisdom, and compassion.

Personal Exploration #18: *Opening to intuition*

If you aren't sure where authenticity would lead you to be, and you have a vague feeling that change is needed, an important first step is to develop greater clarity by learning to access your intuition. First, set your intention to live authentically—that is to say, in service to truth, love, light, God, or whatever ideal speaks to your heart. With that intention in mind, commit to noticing intuitive hints, and to acting on information that you receive. *Acting* doesn't mean that you'll follow incoming messages mindlessly; rather, it means that you'll take your intuitive guidance seriously, that you will earnestly consider whatever arises.

Once you feel drawn towards a specific path, do your research: uncover the details that will help to make your expectations as realistic as possible. This step is essential regardless of the life path choice you are considering—whether you are considering moving to a new city or a new house, getting married, accepting a new job or a promotion, starting a new career, having a baby, or some other major life change.

With well-researched, realistic expectations, visualize your possible path to assess its resonance with your spirit. In this visualization, it's important to be as realistic as possible. For example, if you are considering a career with a smaller income, realistically estimate what the numbers actually say about your future quality of life. Perhaps you'll visualize cooking at home more frequently, having a smaller wardrobe, or taking less extravagant vacations. Perhaps the budget cuts would go far deeper, requiring much larger sacrifices. In the same way, be realistic about your prospective environment. If you are considering a move to Seattle, you'll need to visualize a lot of rain unless you're considering only a brief summer relocation.

Once you have done enough research to have a realistic idea of your contemplated path, find your meditative seat (*Personal Exploration #4: Finding your meditative seat*) and let go of your mental chatter, your *ideas* of how things should be. Next, hold the realistic visualization of a single choice and witness how you feel. If you are weighing two or more choices, visualize them individually, noting how each makes you feel. If I am operating from a clear mind as I compare different opportunities, the inferior choice creates a feeling of contraction somewhere in my body, while the more authentic choice leads to feelings of spaciousness, often focused in my heart.

For this exercise it's essential to quiet your thinking mind first. Otherwise you might feel a contraction created by fear rather than intuition. You may find, like me, that it's the path that creates the most fear in my thinking mind that shines most brightly for my intuition.

I've found that a similar technique works for me if I am feeling out of balance and I don't know what aspect of my life needs the most attention. With a clear mind, I reflect on suspect aspects of my life, visualizing each with as much detail as possible. As I do so, I feel for places of imbalance, being alert to a sudden sense of contraction when I touch on areas that need change.

By softening the grip of certainty, and suspending the belief that you already know how things *are* or *should be*, you create an open-minded, open-hearted approach to challenges, thereby deepening your access to intuition. The increased awareness that accompanies intuition creates the space you need to take the next authentic step into greater personal power.

Embracing crossroads

At the center of your being you have the answer; you know who you are and you know what you want.
—Lao Tzu—

When you are at a crossroad, you may find that you feel weighed down by indecision. The tornado of contrasting thoughts swirling in your mind makes it impossible to connect with your intuition. While you might, at such times, consider doing the preceding exercise, you might also feel certain that the precondition of starting with a quiet mind is an impossibility. You might also be working with so many conflicting thoughts that you can't pick the appropriate possibilities to visualize even if you could quiet your mind. Whenever I find myself in this kind of situation, I've found it can be useful to skillfully work with the thinking mind.

Personal Exploration #19:   Mapping groundwork for change

A valuable first step when contemplating a new path is to truly appreciate your current circumstances. Of course, that doesn't mean that you accept that your current circumstances won't change. It simply means that you start by appreciating as much as you can of whatever is present *right now*. Gratitude is a powerful energy; it opens your heart and mind to the beauty of whatever is present in your life. It creates spaciousness for creativity and empowers opportunities for personal transformation. Moreover, by evaluating with gratitude, you soften the judgmental attitude that can weigh you down like leaded boots, trapping you between what feels like "bad" and "impossible" options.

For this exercise, take out a pen and some paper and write down the following column headings: "Positives," "Negatives," "Strengths," and "Preferences." For this list, the first two columns refer to positive and negative qualities in your *current situation*. The third and fourth columns reflect *you*, regardless of situation. As we work through the worksheet, we'll use the scenario of exploring career choices as an example. But please know that you can easily adapt this exercise to almost any choice you encounter at some personal crossroad.

We'll start with the first two columns. Visualize a work day or, if your work is more variable, each of the types of days you can expect. Do this in as much detail as possible, cataloging everything that feels positive or negative. Remember that your answers will be unique; one person's perfect job is another person's nightmare. So try to let go of generalized judgments about what you *should* like or dislike, and try to record what you actually feel.

Try to describe the positive aspects of your current situation from a perspective of gratitude, identifying the aspects of your current circumstances that serve your needs or feed your spirit. Be honest about the negative aspects. At times, I've found that the very reason that drew me to a particular opportunity became a drawback over time. If you make a similar discovery, put that trait in the "negative" column. These lists should reflect how you feel *right now*, not how you *wish* you felt or *imagined* you would feel when you first accepted the position.

If you are already experiencing burnout, the perspective of gratitude will, paradoxically, be especially valuable in uncovering hidden gifts in your current circumstances. Almost every job has some rewarding aspects. There may be opportunities to develop new skills, serve others, get physical exercise, explore human dynamics, create art, solve business puzzles, or work under conveniently flexible schedules or from any location you choose. There may be people at work whose company you truly enjoy, either coworkers or "the regulars." The salary may be great, or at least good enough to cover your essentials. You may like the location where you work or, perhaps, a park where you can eat lunch. Anything and everything about your working experience can go on that list.

Now that you have detailed the *positives* and *negatives*, review them. It may be that you need to make a big shift in circumstances to align with your authentic path. But in the meantime, are there adjustments that you can make *now* to feel more aligned with your spirit? Can any of your *negatives* be modified by changing something about your work environment, your schedule or your states of mind?

For example, let's say you aren't a morning person, and you roll out of bed at 6:30 a.m. in order to stumble in for a groggy, mandatory 7:00 a.m. clock-in. Can you work a different shift? Or can you give yourself the luxury of time in the morning by waking up 30 or 60 minutes earlier, sipping coffee slowly, and giving yourself time to wake up? Or is it possible for you to exercise first thing, so that you are getting your blood pumping before work begins? If you feel like you spend too much time at your desk, can you adjust your work schedule to add movement? You might, for example, do your brainstorming tasks while walking or meditatively standing in front of a window.

As well, most of us benefit from breaks that feed the spirit. For example, when I worked in Manhattan at an hourly rate, I clocked out daily for a restful and restorative midday break. At times, I'd eat lunch by the water. On other days, I'd meditate in one of the many historic churches downtown. While I couldn't control my exact schedule, I *did* find *some* time every day for quiet reflection in a beautiful space.

Return to your worksheet and fill out the *Strengths* and *Preferences* with your own strengths and preferences. These last two columns tease out qualities that are reflective of *you*, regardless of your circumstances.

They are qualities that you want to bring, or to develop, in your optimal working situation.

Maybe you have a lot of experience, or education, or certifications in some field. If so, those are all strengths. Be sure to catalog any skills developed from hobbies or volunteer work, or from parenting or other caregiving. Personality attributes also go in this column. Write down any aspects of yourself that you feel would allow you to shine in some hypothetical job.

Preferences can include anything about a position: skills you'd like to develop, life situations that you'd like to experience, types of working environments or neighborhoods you'd prefer, salary ranges with which you'd be comfortable, types of people with whom you'd like to interact, roles you'd like to have, the amount of studying you'd need to do to stay current, and more. Give yourself time to relax and reflect as you open your mind and heart to possibility, awakening to your own gifts and drives.

Now that you have a more objective and detailed view of your current job and your current vision of yourself, once again investigate your current circumstances with an eye for change. Many people discover that they find themselves able to renew their appreciation for the opportunities they actually have when they look at their jobs in a fresh light. This is true even for those who feel on the verge of burnout. So, with that in mind, do you have strengths that you aren't using in your current role? Do you have preferences that aren't met? Can you change how you do your job, physically or in terms of your attitudes toward it, in order to better utilize your strengths and satisfy your preferences?

I think it's always a good idea to reflect more broadly about the different roles *others* play in your workplace. Do you see any other positions in your existing workplace that would suit you better? Is there a path to move into those roles? If you've thoroughly investigated your current role, as well as other potential roles, and you still don't see a path towards a good fit, it may be time to broaden the search. Would a similar job at a different company better fit your needs? Or does it feel like you really need to branch out in a completely new direction? Perhaps a new career? Or an entrepreneurial enterprise that grows from your past working experience? Once you discover choices that feel like a good fit, do your research and reflect; confirm that you've found adjustments that will support your personal growth.

Opportunity and luck

You must not let your life run in the ordinary way;
do something that nobody else has done,
something that will dazzle the world.
Show that God's creative principle works in you.
—*Paramahansa Yogananda*—

As you embark on your authentic path, it's essential to keep your eyes, mind, and heart open to unexpected possibilities. By remaining receptive to the new, being willing to change gears, we invite incredible opportunities into our lives. The English researcher, Richard Wiseman, studied two groups of people, those who considered themselves *lucky*, and those who considered themselves *unlucky*. Wiseman found that, in fact, there was no difference between groups in the incidence of purely random events such as winning the lottery or coin tossing contests. Nevertheless, the self-identified lucky people were found to be far happier with their lives in terms of a wide range of indicators, including family life, career success, general health, and finances.

Wiseman found three striking personality differences between the two groups. First, lucky people were more extroverted. By meeting more people, they simply exposed themselves to more positive opportunities. Second, lucky people were less anxious and more relaxed, and therefore were less distracted and more likely to recognize unexpected opportunities when they presented themselves. Third, lucky people were more open to new experiences. Rather than fearing change, they embraced unpredictability while expecting good things to happen. Even in the face of adversity, lucky people turned life's disappointments into new opportunities.

Wiseman then looked into whether people can improve their luck by emulating lucky people. Happily, he found that they can, because lucky people create good fortune via four basic principles. First, they create and notice chance opportunities. While unlucky people tend to follow routines and overlook favorable circumstances, lucky people intentionally introduce variety and change into their lives and keep their eyes open for unexpected possibilities. Second, they make decisions by following their own intuition. Third, they create self-fulfilling prophesies with their positive expectations. Finally, they adopt a resilient attitude that transforms bad luck into good. Wiseman found that lucky people find good luck in part by imagining how it could have been worse. This perspective made them feel blessed, and helped them maintain a positive attitude about the future.

Embracing change and possibility

If it feels like a whole new life is in order, and you aren't sure of the new direction, it is truly useful to read all sorts of sources for inspiration: magazines you aren't normally drawn to that are suddenly appealing, books about unusual places or careers, websites with new ideas. Even if nothing is directly relevant to your new path, simply stepping out of your typical thinking patterns can create a useful shift. It may also be a great time to sign up for new clubs or to volunteer in places that seem somehow intriguing, doing anything that seems like it could get the creative juices flowing. Talk to people in lines at the grocery store or the café, and find out what sorts of opportunities are out there. Realize the vast wealth of knowledge you can tap into by asking other people about their own experiences, and put yourself in the minds of people who may be looking for someone with just your skills and interests.

Once you find your inspiration, do whatever it takes to start on your path, even if it's baby steps. If you feel you need to move overseas, start learning the language and saving money. If you feel drawn to a new career, take online courses in your spare time or volunteer for positions that prepare you in some way for your new direction. Remember that what *they* say you need to start a career is not necessarily true. For example, I have an undergraduate degree in Biology with a minor in Native American Studies, and was able to start a computer consulting career after completing several evening classes in computer programming. There was no need to go back to school and earn a different degree. On the other hand, some careers really do have specific educational requirements for licensing and regulation purposes.

Having an idea of who you are and what you want in terms of where you could most beneficially grow can do wonders in terms of soothing the restlessness associated with dissatisfaction. So long as you are working in the direction of your dream, and so long as you are making some progress along your authentic path, each day brings you closer to making your dream a reality. You'll have extra work to do, but your work will be fueled by the knowledge your life is moving towards expansion, joy, and discovery. By working towards synchronizing your spirit and life circumstances, you'll naturally find a great deal of happiness and peace.

Inviting Transformation

If you do not change direction,
you may end up where you are heading.
—Lao Tzu—

Establishing an environment for growth

Although I have mentioned it before, it bears repeating: *it is easier to wear shoes than to pave the whole world with leather*. I love this saying because it creates a wonderful picture of the tendency to imagine that everything and everyone around us has to change when we sense discomfort in our lives. In fact, the most beneficial change is usually to change our own habitual patterns of thought. As Henry David Thoreau said, "Things do not change; we change."

And yet, it is also valuable to adjust our social, financial, and physical environments in ways that support our finding and walking our authentic paths. When I was taking preparatory classes in anticipation of my Master's program, I was intrigued by reading about the importance of creating an *enabling environment*. One of the women in my class bristled every time she heard the phrase, since she instinctively thought about *enablers*, as in *enabling* substance or domestic abuse. And yet, the authors' intent was to describe creating an empowering environment, an environment conducive to healing. The value of an environment conducive to healing cannot be overstated. And yet, the precise nature of that environment is a razor's edge.

In physical recovery, it's often uncomfortable to work through narrowed ranges of motion after an injury. Once tissue that has lost flexibility has healed enough to permit movement, it takes gentle, consistent effort to slowly regain suppleness. By working gently through the discomfort, your body gradually regains flexibility, becoming in the process much more capable of functioning as you'd like. During the healing process, it's important to recognize that pushing too hard can create a new injury. On the other hand, if you shy from discomfort and avoid working through the stiffness, your body may get tighter, weaker, and more painful.

The path toward personal growth isn't all that different. You may have the urge to have a wholly comfortable environment. You may attempt to create it by surrounding yourself with people who think as you do and who know your buttons well and consciously avoid pushing them. But creating that sort of environmentally-dependent comfort has real drawbacks. It can easily create a feeling of fragility or vulnerability, the sense that you can be happy only so long as life goes according to your whims. As well, you miss the profoundly healing experience of working with your triggers, seeing where you have egoic reactions and investigating the source of each reaction. By exploring a button thoroughly, with no interference from ideas of how you "need" things to be, you have the opportunity to discover that those "should" ideas are insignificant. You can choose to try to be comfortable by hiding from life's challenges, or you can discover something much more important than mere comfort: the contentment of true acceptance, love, gratitude, and peace.

Of course, there is a challenge to finding the right balance in an enabling environment, one that is supportive but not coddling. This balance is, as always, found at the edge: an environment you trust, but that also challenges you sufficiently to grow. Finding your edge is a never-ending process; you must continually adjust the ratio of gentleness to challenge to create the space that invites self-healing. You are discovering what is well, expanding that wellness, working with your edges (whether physical, emotional, social, or some other variety), and creating greater flexibility. You are in the process of developing greater function while simultaneously increasing acceptance and deepening peace. Learning to quiet your mind and to trust your intuition is essential to this practice.

Shifting set points

As a single footstep will not make a path on the earth, so a single thought will not make a pathway in the mind. To make a deep physical path, we walk again and again. To make a deep mental path, we must think over and over the kind of thoughts we wish to dominate our lives.
—Henry David Thoreau—

In medicine, people often talk about *set points*, conditions that your body keeps relatively stable, such as your body temperature. If you've ever dieted, you've probably discovered that your weight similarly has a set point. As you worked hard to shed a few pounds, your body likely worked towards maintaining its weight. We similarly encounter all sorts of set points in our effort to grow in authenticity. We tend to settle into certain relatively narrow ranges of happiness, awareness, and compassion, just as in our physical lives we tend to get comfortable at certain income levels or certain amounts of personal space. To change set points requires will power.

If you've ever decided to stop eating your favorite junk food, you likely found that, at first, your body's cravings grew more and more insistent. But if you remained committed to your new, improved, dietary habits, your cravings eventually quieted down. Ultimately, perhaps, you felt repelled by the junk food you once craved. The process of changing habitual thought patterns works the same way. At first it feels like a herculean effort to consistently commit to a new way of thinking. But persistent effort truly pays off. It provides the power you need to shift your set points in thinking. Over time, by consistently embracing more mindful modes of thinking, it becomes more natural and effortless to live your life guided by wisdom and compassion. Moreover, you'll find greater success if you apply steady, purposeful effort instead of yo-yoing back and forth between intensity and laxity on your journey.

Transformation on your authentic path

Walking a path that resonates authentically with your spirit is empowering: it gives you the energy and drive you need to make beneficial shifts. As you grow more and more aligned with your authentic path, you'll see old set points dissolve and new ones form. It is, however, important to understand that self-discovery is rarely a steady, gradual process. On the contrary, personal growth is usually like the graphs describing *punctuated equilibrium*, with cycles of level periods followed by abrupt change.

Level periods have many causes. Sometimes, after a period of growth, you may feel yourself falling into self-congratulatory inattention. Or you might be spinning your wheels, working busily but counterproductively, investing your energy in ways that are not aligned with your path. You might also be on the verge of discovery, but afraid of what you may find about yourself or your life. On the other hand, if you are truly applying focused effort, and it is truly in alignment with your path, you might simply be storing up the potential energy that will eventually blast you to your next level of understanding.

As always, honest self-reflection is essential to understand the cause of a period of apparent stagnation. For this reflection, you'll let your thoughts be as they are, not believing them, or arguing with them, but simply trying to see them clearly and to hold them in a compassionate field of energy. Let thoughts of *should have, could have, would have* dissolve. Trust your intuition to see where you need to adjust, and where you need to redouble your efforts. You may find that you need the counsel of a trusted spiritual guide, psychologist, or friend. Having people you can count on for honest, compassionate insight is invaluable. Even so, you'll still need to reflect, question, and feel for yourself rather than adopting others' perspectives unquestioningly.

Know that life is a process, and that we are always *in progress*. If you notice that you are out of alignment with your truth, there is no need to beat yourself up. In fact, that's counterproductive. As the Buddha said, "You, yourself, as much as anybody in the entire universe, deserve your love and affection." Simply lovingly, mindfully, and wisely notice where you need readjustment, and make the change.

Once you have found your new direction, it's essential to reflect on your status to ensure that you are still on a path that feels authentic for you. Sometimes we are lulled into complacency when no crisis is present. Sometimes we put forth wonderful effort to reveal our paths, but then lose discipline in walking them. Consistency in applying awareness, focused effort, acceptance, and compassion is essential. To truly walk *your* authentic path, you must also align your life towards *your* life's purpose, letting go of thoughts, activities, and relationships that are not in alignment with your truth. Since we are all, by nature, creatures of habit, this shedding process can be the most challenging aspect of living authentically.

Personal Exploration #20: ***Releasing ideas of progress and stasis***

If I am feeling restless, feeling like I'm not progressing fast enough, or getting too far ahead of myself, I find it valuable to perform a meditation that offers those thoughts inquisitive compassion. For this exploration, first perform the preliminary steps (*Personal Exploration #4: Finding your meditative seat*), finding a comfortable seat of balance, and resting in a field of non-judgmental awareness. Holding this loving, spacious awareness, meditate on questions like, *What if it's never enough? What if there is no final destination? What if this is as good as it gets? Can you still open fully, with joy, to what's here now?*

Anyone who's had a spiritual practice probably knows the "right" answers to those questions. But, this isn't a test, and the "right" answers are not terribly useful in themselves. Instead, give your thoughts compassionate space, and see what truly arises. You may want to create a list. *What if it's never enough?* What does that mean? What fears arise for you with that thought? Recognize what arises, without guilt or blame or argument. Welcome it with loving, spacious awareness, and see what happens. This meditation can open incredible doors of peace and understanding, but only if you are willing to courageously rest in loving awareness (and abandon lofty thought).

Stepping beyond *should*

One of the most powerful lines for me in *The Matrix* was spoken by Morpheus when he was teaching Neo martial arts. After easily dodging several strikes, Morpheus said, "Quit *trying* to hit me and *hit* me." Everyone has likely had the experience of *trying* to do something so intently that it is impossible to actually do it. For example, there is a world of difference between *trying* to meditate and *meditating*. The fundamental problem is that *trying* points to the future, while *doing* happens in the present. In *The Matrix*, Neo was *trying* to hit Morpheus, a process that involved a delay between thought and action. A thousand thoughts about technique and strategy, or winning and losing, or costs and opportunities, can swirl in a moment. These thoughts take you right out of the immediacy of your experience.

In the context of self-discovery, it is far too easy to get lost in a sea of should; you *should* open to Stillness, you *should* feel the interconnectedness of everyone and everything, you *should* be insightful… All of these *shoulds* point to some *future, better time* for some *future, better you*. I invite you to be *you*, just as you are, beyond any *ideas* of who you are, or who you should be. I invite you to rest in your ground of mindfulness and acceptance while opening your heart to possibility.

Love, life, and change

One of the things I find interesting about the endocrine system is that there are two basic types of hormones: those that dissolve in water (the hydrophilic hormones), and those that don't (the lipid-soluble hormones). While the lipid-soluble hormones can pass right into a cell, directing the cell's creation of new proteins directly, the hydrophilic hormones can't actually enter their target cells at all. Instead, they sit on the cell's surface, changing the cell's configuration. This shift causes changes inside the cell, resulting in the creation of vast numbers of chemical messengers. In time, a single hydrophilic hormone's binding to a single cell receptor might activate (or, deactivate) millions of enzymes within the cell. When its work is done, the hormone floats away.

That process is metaphorically similar to the way situations or people sometimes appear in our lives. Sometimes we seek out something that we intuitively know we need to discover or explore. Sometimes, someone or something new appears. Or someone we've known for a long time, or an opportunity that's been available for quite a while, suddenly shines in a new light. As we adjust to meet the external change, we experience a dramatic cascade of internal shifts and their outward expression.

It's easy in those cases to get attached to whatever we imagine generated the internal blossoming. For example, when people fall in love, they often imagine that all of the joy that arises is caused by the other person. From that perspective, it's easy to imagine that if that person changes or leaves, love is lost. But in reality, the joy of love is due to the feeling of expansion that is inherent in loving.

A relationship can morph from the joyous *budding love* stage to the deeper, quieter *deeply loving* stage. And if you let go of wanting things always to be the way they used to be, it's easy to experience how perfect things are, just as they are. Sometimes love morphs completely, into more of a friendship, and dating no longer makes sense. The nature of the relationship has shifted, and the partner connected to it has somehow changed into something more like a sibling. Although there's still lots of room for love there, it also becomes important to learn how to live the relationship in an authentic way. Sometimes, like a hormone molecule that has delivered its message and detaches from the recipient cell, the parties to a relationship need to see the purpose of the relationship has been realized, and it's time to part ways. This change, too, can be lived authentically and lovingly.

I find that there is also a sort of activation for me that is associated with life events. For example, when I started college, I loved the academic rigors. I was planning to go right from a BA program to an MD program. But as senior year came, it felt important to seek a new kind of challenge. So right after college, I moved out to New York City to start my career. At first, it was exciting and, frankly, taxing. Many transformations were necessary, including adapting to living in a crowded city, understanding how to dress and act professionally, learning new job skills, and being responsible for my expenses. After I had lived on the East Coast for several years, I built up a solid career in Information Technology. But then I felt a new pull and headed out to Colorado, developing a completely different lifestyle. And as I mentioned before, another big shift occurred when my dog was diagnosed.

My various life phases have been incredibly beneficial; each offered incredible opportunities to explore and discover. And yet clinging to any of them for the sake of routine would have been a mistake. When I felt a phase dropping away from me, it felt a lot more authentic to close it out properly, taking care to complete my responsibilities before moving on, while mapping out and stepping into the next step of personal evolution.

So I encourage you to find the dance that matches your authentic cosmic rhythms. The most essential skill to sense your authentic direction is the ability to quiet your thinking mind and feel with your heart for transformational opportunities—without worrying about the way the ego thinks things should look on the outside. In other words ask, yourself *What would Love do?* and then step into that space.

Conscious and unconscious competence

A wonderful karate teacher with whom I trained in Boulder frequently talked about the four levels of competency in the context of martial arts. This way of viewing learning is insightful; it is relevant to learning most skills, including meditation and mindfulness. In this paradigm, the levels are as follows:

Unconscious incompetence: When you begin to learn a new skill, you may throw yourself into the practice blissfully unaware of your incompetence. You are having fun, exploring, and taking in new information. You are not worrying about outcomes. If you are in an art class, you are celebrating colors as they spread across the canvas. If you are learning yoga, you are enjoying the feel of your body moving in new ways without giving too much thought to form. If you are journaling, you are enjoying words as they appear at the tip of your pen without worrying about their value to others.

This is the *beginning phase*, the *dabbler's phase*, where everything is new and joyful, and it is great fun. You might choose to remain a dabbler in some activities, for the sheer fun of it. For example, I rarely bowl, but when I do, it's simply a social activity for me. I am not interested in developing bowling skills. Instead, I simply enjoy bowling as a relaxing pastime with friends. On the other hand, this stage isn't terribly useful for skills that you hope to hone. Since you don't notice where you could improve, you don't have much to work with in refining your techniques.

Conscious incompetence: In this stage, you begin to notice that your techniques have a ways to go, and you realize that developing competence will take more focused intent. In a beginning meditation practice, at this *conscious incompetence* stage, you start noticing the innumerable thoughts zipping by. You might even wonder if meditation is actually *causing* increased mental activity. In art class, you notice that your paintings are displeasing to you in some way, unbalanced, disproportionate, or drab, and you realize you don't know how to create what you see in your mind's eye. In snowboarding, you are increasingly aware of how many times you wipe out.

This stage is hard on the ego, and it's usually when most people drop out. The fun of unconscious incompetence has become a distant memory, and the joys of the next stage have yet to be discovered. Although you feel frustrated, this can be a very productive time if you stick it out. You are noticing where techniques require improvement, and you are starting to understand concepts that are essential for learning your new skill.

Conscious competence: At this stage practice starts getting really fun again. You have a much better understanding of subtle skills and techniques, and you are constantly refining your craft. You see what makes your techniques effective, and you study and refine them for further improvements. In painting, you consciously engage the skills and insights that are necessary to create a compelling image. In snowboarding, you gracefully carve down mountains, aware of where you need to direct subtle shifts as you move. In meditation, you notice when your mind drifts and you bring it back to your point of focus.

Growth requires that we know both what we do well and what we need to improve. So, the best learners shift between conscious incompetence and conscious competence. They combine mental and physical investigation with mental and physical practices, developing increasingly greater skill.

Unconscious competence: There are two very different possibilities at this stage. On one hand, you might circle back to the beginning, imagining yourself to be an expert and consequently becoming sloppy and inattentive. As training takes a progressively more distant back seat to mental wandering, you revert to unconscious incompetence, making mistakes you don't even notice or notice only after it's too late to correct them.

On the other hand, this stage could also describe the state of *Mushin*, where there is no time and no mind, no ego, and no need to do anything in particular. In the state of *Mushin*, you are completely present and flow perfectly into whatever is happening in the moment. Rather than *thinking* (which points to the future), you intuitively *feel* what is actually happening. You replace the delay of mental processing with the immediacy of intuition, and "should" no longer exists. There is simply "Is." Experience is met directly, and action occurs without hesitation. The state of *Mushin* is the objective in many martial arts and meditation practices. Of course, the broader intent is that your whole life becomes permeated with *Mushin,* not simply the moments of training or combat.

Competence within a mindfulness practice

Meditation and spiritual practice more generally have these same stages. Once in a seminar, a Tibetan Rinpoche gave us twenty minutes to count, and then asked us how high we were able to count. The catch was that, if our minds wandered from counting for even a moment, we had to start over at one. After twenty minutes had passed, he asked us to call out our numbers. I've forgotten now what numbers people called out, but I remember his laughing pretty hard and saying, "You guys are way too easy on yourselves!" We were in that first stage of *unconscious incompetence*, not even noticing our minds' wanderings.

After you have been practicing meditation for a period of time, especially if you are also doing the sort of mindfulness training that requires watching the mind's activities, you'll break through into the *conscious incompetence* phase. At this point, people sometimes complain that they are actually thinking far *more* than they did before trying to meditate, and they quit. The truth, however, is that they are simply now noticing the mental static that they've ignored for most of their lives. If they had continued to work through this phase, they would have discovered the satisfaction of *conscious competence*.

When you are crossing a stream, your boots are going to get wet. But if you really want to get to the other shore, don't let the discomfort keep you from the warm campfire and friendship on the other side. When you start a new meditation practice, your thoughts often seem louder at first because you are starting to notice them more. If you stick with the practice, that chatter will eventually settle down. As well, your *monkey mind's* ability to draw you into following your thoughts (rather than simply noticing thoughts and letting them pass) will diminish considerably. This is the point at which you get to experience the fun of the *conscious competence* phase, where your learning and development blooms. You study what you know and what you need to refine, working intently and consciously. You may shift between the second and third stages of learning for a long time, studying, developing, and deepening your practice.

At some point though, you may drift into the *unconscious competence* phase. Just as in martial arts, it's important to be aware that there is a world of difference between the two different expressions of this phase. While one will make you feel dull, disconnected, or sloppy, the other makes you feel bright, joyful, connected, and in tune with the Flow. If you find yourself dully and unconsciously competent, whether in martial arts, meditation, or life, it's important to notice and to choose again to live consciously, trusting that, eventually, your conscious attention will transform into *Mushin*, the most profound form of unconscious competence.

Personal Exploration #21: Exploring competence

Choose an activity for which you have at least moderate capability. See how well you can sort your skills into levels of competence.

- Can you discern specific skills for which you know you need to develop greater competency?
- Can you identify skills for which you are aware of your high level of proficiency?
- Even trickier, while engaged in the activity, can you observe yourself sufficiently well to identify missing skills that previously escaped your attention? That is, can you make conscious what was previously unconscious incompetence?
- On the other hand, can you remember moments when you've been so engaged in the activity that it simply felt as if the activity was flowing through you, that *being* and *action* had merged into in a single, flawless dance?

After reflecting on skills that fit into each level, consider: What level or levels of competence do you mostly perform at when engaged in your selected activity?

Continual refinement

You likely have heard the familiar phrase, *Practice makes perfect*. But that expression is a little misleading because practice simply reinforces patterns. If your practice is sloppy, practice makes sloppiness. In martial arts teachers speak of *kaizen*, which translates roughly as *continual refinement*. Certainly, repetition aids in learning new skills.

But the key is *kaizen,* consciously making whatever you practice more perfect with every repetition. You could also say, *Perfect practice makes perfect.*

My Shotokan karate teacher believed in the power of repetition. He'd have us do a few hundred punches in a row on most days. It's easy, when you are doing the same thing so many times, to lose track of the task. The mind and the body easily get bored and so overlook the nuances that transform an arm in the air into a grounded punch. The key is to stay fully present. Each strike is the only punch. It is performed as perfectly as possible and is quickly assessed for whatever needs refinement. The next punch becomes the only strike. The refinements in it are applied, and the punch is assessed for more fine-tuning.

Mindfulness similarly entails observing the mind's running commentary, such as about physical sensations or states of mind. In watching the mind without being judgmental, we can see where we leave the present as, for example, when we wish we didn't need to drive to work or wash the dishes, or that the weather or other people were somehow different, or in fretting about possible events in our future. In honestly assessing where we are being judgmental, we have the opportunity to release those judgments, experiencing the situation or person directly, meeting them *as they are.*

Personal Exploration #22:   Consciously performing everyday tasks

Choose a task that you find dully repetitive. This could be a household task, such as vacuuming, scrubbing the floor, or doing dishes. Or it might be an outside job like mowing the yard or grocery shopping. You might also choose a task at work, like scheduling and making phone calls or answering email.

As you do the task, see how consciously aware of your activity you can be. Notice where you can refine your performance. If you are cleaning, work towards staying fully present with each swipe of your sponge. If you are driving, work towards being aware of where each car is positioned, and where it is going. If you are making calls at work, try to infuse each interaction with compassionate presence.

Truly explore the nuances of your "boring" task, and see just how deeply engaging and meditative it can be.

Season of transition

"Don't worry that your life is turning upside down.
How do you know that the side you are used to
is better than the one to come?"
—Rumi—

When I lived in California, I found there wasn't a huge difference between summer and winter. In Colorado, I love experiencing the sweeping seasonal changes. The unpredictability of spring in Colorado can be captivating. Once, my mom visited in May on a day that shifted from 80 degrees and sunny to well below freezing and snowing in just 10 hours. In Colorado, our summer days can range from mild to hot, and from sunny to storming and hailing. Our winters get pretty cold and snowy, but we also get many gorgeous, cool, sunny days.

In autumn, the bright green leaves gradually shift through golds, oranges, and browns, and drift to the ground in brightly colored piles, some crunchy and some soft and fragrant, releasing the unmistakable scent of fall when underfoot. Some of the flowering plants draw their nutrients inward, fading and melting back into the earth in anticipation of the cold. Others continue to bloom, celebrating the tail-end of the growth season, putting out one last colorful display before temperatures dip below freezing. Mornings often begin with a thin, shimmering layer of frost on leaves, sparkling in the soft morning sunlight.

There are aspects of fall that provide natural continuity between summer and winter. For example, average temperatures drop as you'd expect, and plant materials gradually become winter compost. Even so, autumn is a distinctly different season with its own smells, colors, and sounds that you might never guess if you were asked to imagine a season that connects the baking, bright sun and lush foliage of summer to the frigid, sparkling snow and stark landscapes of winter.

Often, we try to imagine connecting temporal points A and B, whether it's through time looking backwards (perhaps interpreting past events and wondering how a life ended up at its current crossroad) or out into the future (evaluating possible paths that just might get you to point B). And our "reality" and our imaginings about how things *should* be are a little—or very—divergent. And yet, there is such beauty in how things unfold, just as they are… just as, with fall, we enjoy cold nights, slimy, fragrant leaves, perfect blue skies, and incredible displays of color.

At times in my life, I've struggled against the changing of *my* seasons, clinging to leaves that were ready to fall, or attempting to will fruits to ripen before they were ready. For example, when working at an enjoyable job that no longer felt like an authentic fit, I've tried at times to *cling to my leaves*, making myself smaller, squeezing into a position even after my intuitive voice suggested I needed to expand my horizons. Or, when I've burned with the discomfort of a job that became too confining, I've tried to pry open other opportunities that simply needed love, light, and a little more time to ripen naturally.

When I sense internal struggles against my own changing seasons, I've found it profoundly useful to notice, and to provide that struggle with recognition and space. I've also found it tremendously beneficial to soften into what is here *right now*, without fretting about my grand plans and roadmaps. What beauty to consciously take each step: reflecting, sensing, and knowing that you are truly welcoming your current season— whether it is a season of new growth, expansion, storage, or rest—and that you are simultaneously consciously shaping authentic change.

As you embrace your authentic path, guided by mindfulness, wisdom, and compassion, I hope you celebrate the transitions. I hope you come to appreciate and love the fleeting moments of shifting possibility that unfold beautifully, unpredictably, and exquisitely into your authentic life. I wish you tremendously well on your journey as you discover, explore, and deepen in joy.

Namaste
The Spirit and Light within me
honors and celebrates
the Spirit and Light in you.

Additional materials

If you would like to further explore *Joy's Edge*, please visit http://www.joysedge.com/resources to find additional materials, such as audio recordings of meditations and supplemental exercises.